Making the Most of the One-Computer Classroom
Grades K-6

By: Concetta Doti Ryan, M.A.

Illustrated by Scott Bricher

Permissions: Graphics/images courtesy of Kid Pix Studio - 1994, 1995, 1996 Brøderbund Software, Inc. All rights reserved. Used by permission. Kid Pix Studio and Brøderbund are trademarks and/or registered trademarks of Brøderbund Software, Inc.

HyperStudio© is registered trademark of Roger Wagner Publishing, Inc.

Screen Shots from System 8.1© 1983–1997 Apple Computer, Inc. Used with permission.
ClarisWorks software Copyright 1991–1997 Apple Computer, Inc.
Apple® and the Apple logo, and *ClarisWorks* are trademarks of Apple Computer, Inc., registered in the U.S. and other countries. All Rights Reserved.

At the time of printing *ClarisWorks software* is named *AppleWorks software*.

Project Manager: Barbara G. Hoffman
Editor: Donna Borst
Book Design: Anthony D. Paular
Cover Design: Anthony D. Paular
Pre-Press Production: Daniel Willits

FS123298 Making the Most of the One-Computer Classroom Grades K–6
All rights reserved—Printed in the U.S.A.
23740 Hawthorne Blvd.
Torrance, CA 90505

Notice! Pages may be reproduced for classroom or home use only, not for commercial resale. No part of this publication may be reproduced for storage in a retrieval system, or transmitted in any form or by any means—electronic, mechanical, recording, etc.—without the prior written permission of the publisher. Reproduction of these materials for an entire school or school system is strictly prohibited.

SCHWARTING SCHOOL LIBRARY

Copyright © 1999 Frank Schaffer Publications, Inc.

Table of Contents

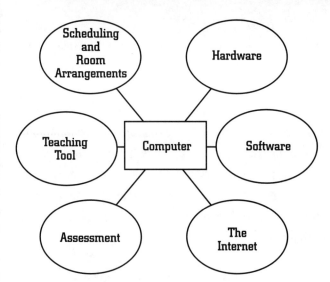

This book was written for teachers who want to know if there is anything they can do with only one computer in their classrooms. The answer is an emphatic YES! This book is filled with things you can do with just one computer. After reading this book you should feel confident that you can add a wonderfully rich technology component to your curriculum with just one computer. Additionally, the basic tutorials will help you learn how to operate basic word processing, paint, spreadsheet, and multimedia software. Take a look at the resources you will find in this book.

- Ideas for making the most of whatever technology you have in your classroom, even if it is just one computer, are offered in detail. You will read about several different ways to use the computer you have. It can be used as a learning center or publishing center. It can also be used by groups of students in a cooperative learning exercise.

- Management ideas such as scheduling students for computer time are presented along with sample schedules you can follow to create your own schedule for your classroom.

- Sample room arrangements are provided.

- The book also contains information on computer basics as well as how to use some of the most popular software for elementary classrooms. Though the instructions are for specific software, many of the functions work the

same way in all software of that type. For example, once you learn how to format text in *ClarisWorks*, you should be able to format text in any word processing software, because they all work pretty much the same. Once you learn how to use the paint tools in *Kid Pix Studio* or *Kid Pix Studio Deluxe*, you should be able to use these tools in most other pieces of paint software and so on.

- A discussion of how to introduce a software program to students is provided on page 13. You can follow these steps for introducing any piece of software. Information about how to project what you are doing on your computer onto a large screen can be found on page 13.

- There is also information on assessment. Two assessment options are included to help you do either a quantitative or qualitative assessment. A sample checklist is provided on page 16, and a sample rubric is included on page 17.

- If you are interested in the Internet and its vast resources, you will enjoy reading pages 18-20. Terrific sites for teachers are also included. You should visit these and check out the wealth of information available online for teachers.

- Finally, there are lots of curriculum ideas for integrating technology. The activity ideas are divided into four content areas. You will find project ideas as well as detailed lesson plans on pages 30-78.

Learning centers have been used by teachers in primary classrooms for years. Some activities that students complete at learning centers are designed to practice and reinforce skills. Because students are already familiar with the skills, they can complete the practice activities at the centers on their own.

Traditional classroom learning centers include a reading center, a writing center, a math center, a science center, a listening center, and an art center. Now that you have a computer in the classroom, students have the opportunity to enjoy a whole new center! A computer learning center encourages students to familiarize themselves with the computer and practice a variety of skills on their own.

Student Rotation

Students move to the computer learning center just as they do to the other centers in your classroom. If the computer is the only center you will be using, then schedule the students in 25-minute blocks throughout the week. If you find that you do not have enough time to give each students a 25-minute block, try using 20-minute blocks, or have the students work in pairs. You will find a discussion about scheduling and some sample schedules on pages 5-8. If parent volunteers or older students are available, ask them to be "computer buddies" at your center. These "buddies" can help familiarize your class with the computer and the particular software, and they can also help move students to the center.

Center Management

When designing activities for the computer learning center, keep in mind that they will probably have to be completed in 15 to 20 minutes in order to keep the learning center rotation on schedule. Students should be introduced to computer basics and the standard operation of the software before they are sent to the computer learning center to complete an activity. When students understand the basics of computer and software use, then they will be able to concentrate on the assigned activity. For tips on teaching technology to students, see page 14.

Sometimes students will be unable to complete the assigned activity within 20 minutes. In these cases, students should be told which part of the activity they should complete by the end of the first session and what is expected during the second session. This will keep students on track.

Have a place where students put their completed work. Teach students how to quit or exit the software program prior to leaving the computer learning center, to ensure that the computer is ready for the next student.

You may want to consider using your computer as a publishing center. Word processing software is a powerful tool for editing and publishing student writing.

Have you ever noticed that when students know they are going to be writing a story that will go through the writing process, their stories become much shorter and less creative? The reasons for this are obvious. If they are going to have to rewrite the story over and over again, it stands to reason that they will want to write as short a story as possible. The ease with which editing can be accomplished with word processing software eliminates this damper on creativity. Students know how simple it is to make a change, be it a simple spelling correction or moving an entire paragraph. Both are a simple click away!

When using the computer as a publishing center, you might want to investigate the use of portable keyboards. If students use all their computer time to type, they are not getting to use the computer for more advanced applications. Portable keyboards solve this problem. Students type their stories into the portable keyboard. Then, the story is downloaded (a very simple process) into the computer for formatting and editing. These portable keyboards are both Macintosh and PC compatible. Schools often invest in a class set that can be checked out by teachers when their students need to enter a large amount of text.

An alternative method to input stories is to request a parent volunteer to do the first-draft word processing.

Once students have the text in the computer, they can use the powerful publishing tools available with most word-processing software. Students can use the spell check and thesaurus to assist with the mechanics of a story. They can also use formatting features which allow them to improve the look of their work. When students format the text, they can change the font (type style of the text), size of the font, style of the font (bold, italics, or underline), and alignment (left aligned, centered, or right aligned). Most word processing software will also allow students to add graphics to their stories. Some, like *ClarisWorks* have a selection of built-in graphics. Others allow students to import graphics created in a painting program such as *ClarisWorks* or *Kid Pix Studio* or *Kid Pix Studio Deluxe* into the word processing document.

All of these features allow students to create an attractive hard copy of their personal writing. Students can print out and share their work with the class either orally or by posting their writing on a bulletin board. Or, students can publish their work online by using the Internet.

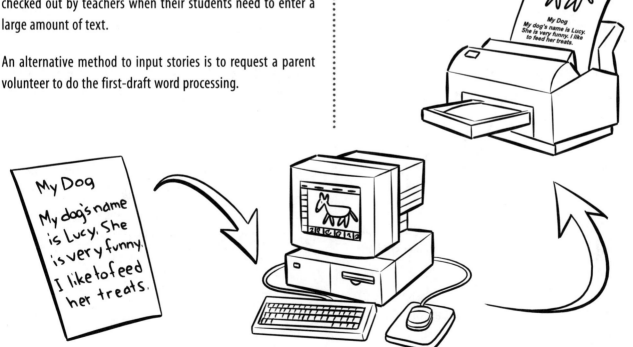

If you have one computer and a limited amount of time in which students can use it, you could consider having them work at the computer with a partner. This enables you to emphasize several learning outcomes. Students will learn computer skills, practice content skills, and work on their cooperative learning skills by completing activities and projects with a partner.

Even if your schedule allows students to work at the computer for 20 minutes each week, you may have an activity that requires more time at the computer, or an activity that you would like done with a partner. If you schedule students at the computer in pairs, then they have 40 rather than 20 minutes to complete an activity.

For years we have heard about the benefits of cooperative learning. Below are just a few.

"Cooperative learning situations tend to promote higher achievement than do competitive or individualistic learning situations." (Psychological Bulletin, Volume 89, 1981)

"Cooperative learning situations promote positive social outcomes such as leadership ability, communication, and conflict management skills." (Circles of Learning, Interaction Book Company, 1984)

"Cooperative learning helps students develop the ability to adjust in social situations, trust and optimism in peers, basic self-acceptance, and positive self-esteem." (Journal of Social Psychology, Volume 120, 1983)

"Students who work together cooperatively toward a common goal find themselves developing an appreciation for the strengths in others." (Journal of Special Education, Volume 17, 1983)

The computer is an excellent tool for developing cooperative skills as students work together on a computer project. Not only do students perceive working together as fun, they can coach each other as they conduct electronic research using an electronic encyclopedia or the Internet. Two heads are better than one, when you're researching a topic. Students can also play learning games together. There is excellent software available that teaches content skills within a "game" environment – highly motivating for students!

Whether you choose to have students work at the computer cooperatively because you are short on time or because you want to promote social learning, the results are the same. Even if you don't always have students work together, you may want to present some activities for student pairs.

You are not alone if you have a computer in your classroom that is used in a haphazard way. Some weeks, each student has time to work on it. Other weeks, it just sits there unused. Typically, it is used at holiday time so students can make cards. You want students to use it on a regular basis, but you just never quite get around to it because you are so busy with teaching content lessons. Does all of this sound familiar?

If you set a schedule for weekly computer use, chances are your students will stick to that schedule. You are probably wondering how setting a schedule will change the complexities, disruptions, and busy classroom schedule. It won't. However, if students know that they have a special time to use the computer on their own, they won't let you forget. This time is precious to them. The computer is very motivating and downright fun to use. Once you set that schedule, you'll be amazed to see students quietly getting up from their seats at their assigned time. They don't forget!

Setting the schedule can be somewhat difficult. Try to give students 20-minute sessions at the computer. There are few activities that can be completed in less time than that. If you can afford 30 or 40 minutes, that is even better, particularly if you are planning to use the computer for projects that involve a lot of word processing. (See hints for dealing with slow keyboarding on page 3.)

The sample schedules included on pages 6 through 8 were developed based on a class of 30 students. Look at your daily teaching schedule. At what points during the day can you slot in 20-minute computer blocks? Isn't it amazing how easy it is to come up with four to six 20-minute blocks during the day? If you do have trouble finding four to six 20-minute blocks, try scheduling students to work at the computer in pairs. There is a sample cooperative group schedule on page 8. By pairing students, you only need two to three 20-minute blocks each day. We can all find that amount of time! Once you make your schedule, see where you can increase computer time to 30 or 40-minute blocks. These extra minutes will enable students to accomplish much more.

You may also want to schedule a make-up session during the week. This is for students who were absent or who missed their regular sessions because special school activities, like assemblies, occurred during their assigned computer time. This way, you can be sure that every student has the opportunity to complete the computer project. You may also want to set a policy for students who miss their computer time because they forget. Do you allow them to use the make-up session? Will they need to miss recess or stay after school to make up the time? Or, will they simply not be graded on the assignment? This is something you should think about before the situation arises so students know the consequences in advance.

Once your schedule is set, inform your students. Emphasize that it is their responsibility to remember their times. You will not be reminding them. Be sure that they understand what will happen if they miss their computer time.

You will find sample schedules and room arrangements on the next few pages.

Sample Schedule #1

The following schedule is based on the assumption that each student will work at the computer for a 20-minute session and that you have 30 students in your class. Notice that instructional time has been blocked out. This schedule can be used if you want students to work at the computer once a week or if you use it as a learning center.

	Mon	Tue	Wed	Thu	Fri
8:30-8:45	Introduction				
8:45-9:30	Language Arts Instruction				
9:30-9:50	Steve	Michele	Jose	Natalie	Twan
9:50-10:15	Recess				
10:15-11:00	Math Instruction				
11:00-11:20	Megan	Bryce	Tori	Heath	Juanita
11:20-11:40	Jason	Melanie	Austin	Vicky	Brady
11:40-12:00	Patty	Erik	Jia	John	Amanda
12:00-12:45	Lunch				
12:45-1:00	Silent Reading				
1:00-1:20	Sean	Maria	Tim	Brianna	Arthur
1:20-1:40	Jessie	Mark	Susan	Joel	Kristin
1:40-2:30	Social Studies or Science Instruction				
2:30-3:00	Closing				

FS123298 Making the Most of the One-Computer Classroom © Copyright Frank Schaffer Publications, Inc.

The following schedule is based on the assumption that each student will work at the computer for a 30-minute session and that you have 30 students in your class. Notice that instructional time in language arts and math has been blocked out. This schedule can be used if you want students to work at the computer once a week or if you use it as a learning center.

	Mon	Tue	Wed	Thu	Fri
8:30-8:45	Introduction				
8:45-9:30	Language Arts Instruction				
9:30-10:00	Jessie	Mark	Susan	Joel	Kristin
10:00-10:30	Steve	Michele	Jose	Natalie	Twan
10:30-10:45	Recess				
10:45-11:30	Math Instruction				
11:30-12:00	Megan	Bryce	Tori	Heath	Juanita
12:00-12:45	Lunch				
12:45-1:00	Silent Reading				
1:00-1:30	Sean	Maria	Tim	Brianna	Arthur
1:30-2:00	Patty	Erik	Jia	John	Amanda
2:00-2:30	Jason	Melanie	Austin	Vicky	Brady
2:30-3:00	Closing				

Sample Schedule #3

The following schedule is based on the assumption that each student will work at the computer for a 40-minute session and that you have 30 students in your class. Notice that instructional time has been blocked out. This schedule can be used if you want students to work at the computer once a week or if you use it as a learning center.

	Mon	Tue	Wed	Thu	Fri
8:30-8:45	Introduction				
8:45-9:30	Language Arts Instruction				
9:30-10:10	Jessie/Mark	Susan/Joel	Kristin/Steve	Michele/Jose	Natalie/Twan
10:10-10:30	Recess				
10:30-11:15	Math Instruction				
11:15-11:55	Megan/Bryce	Tori/Heath	Juanita/Sean	Maria/Tim	Brianna/Arthur
11:55-12:40	Lunch				
12:40-1:00	Silent Reading				
1:00-1:40	Patty/Erik	Jia/John	Amanda/Jason	Melanie/Austin	Vicky/Brady
1:40-2:30	Social Studies or Science Instruction				
2:30-3:00	Closing				

 FS123298 Making the Most of the One-Computer Classroom © Copyright Frank Schaffer Publications, Inc.

There are some important points to consider prior to determining your room arrangement. Direct sun, water, and chalk dust can harm your computer, so keep it away from the windows, the sink, and the chalkboard. It needs to be near an electrical outlet and the phone line if you want to connect to the Internet. You should also place the computer away from heavy traffic areas and in a location where students will not be distracted by activity on the screen while they are supposed to be working on something else.

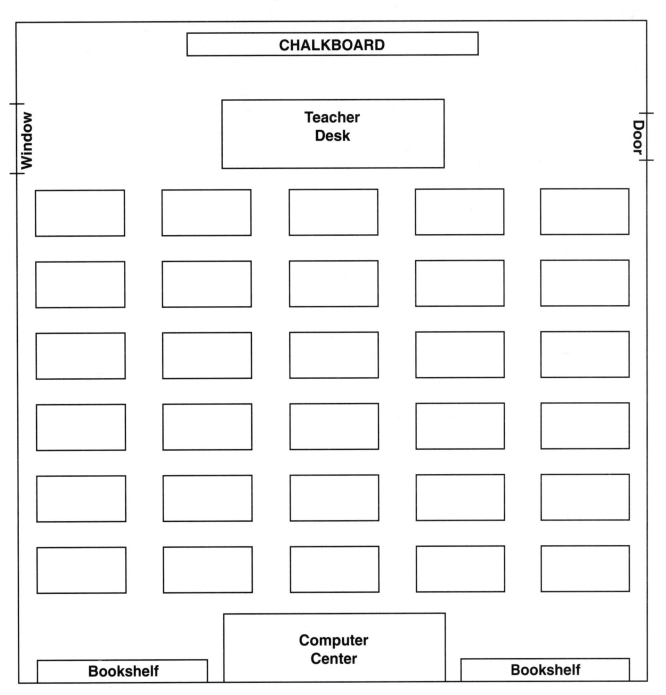

Sample Room Arrangement #2

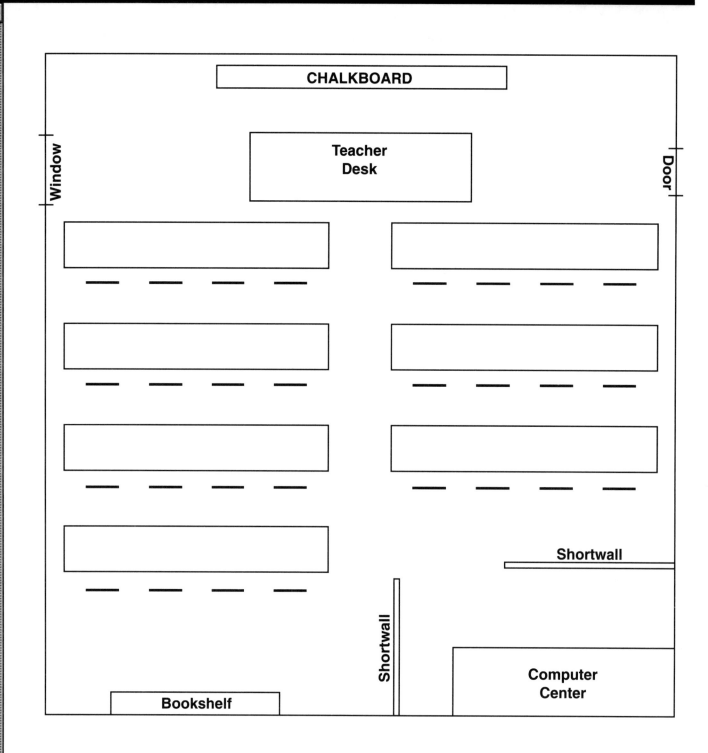

CHALKBOARD

Window

Door

Teacher Desk

Shortwall

Shortwall

Bookshelf

Computer Center

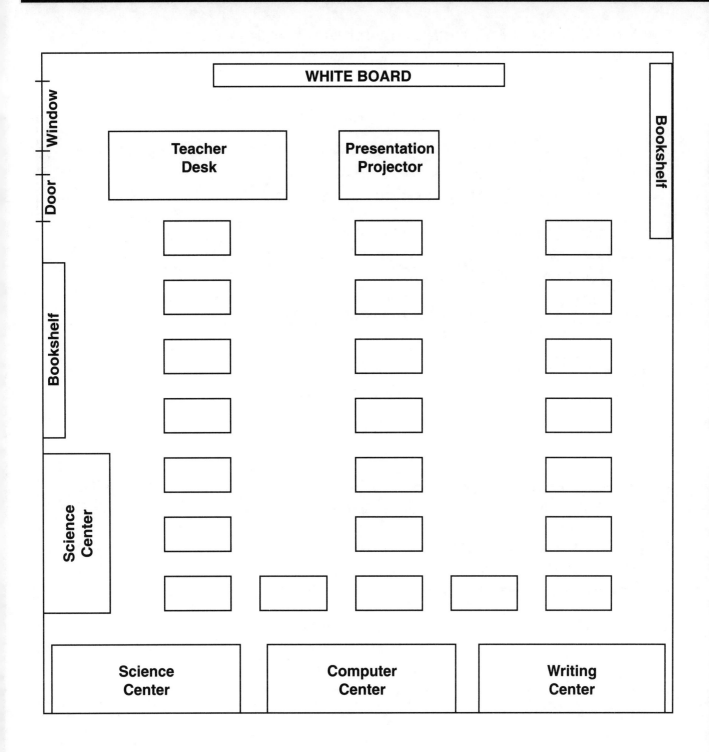

1. At the end of each activity card there is a step asking students to quit, or exit, the program. Students are asked to do this so the computer is always ready for the next student.

2. Students should understand that when their computer time is over, they should immediately leave the computer.

3. Students should take all their materials away from the computer area when they are finished. The area should be left the way they found it, or neater!

4. Students should always type their names on their work. Undoubtedly, students will not have enough time to wait for their projects to print. If their names are on their work, papers can be distributed to the rightful owners at a later time.

5. If students are allowed to wait for their work to print, designate an area where they turn in their work after they have looked at it.

6. If students are working with software that has sound, they should be taught how to adjust the volume. Consider headphones for student use at the computer.

7. Introduce software to students prior to sending them to the computer center to use it.

8. If you are using the computer as a center, review your rules for the other learning centers and explain that all these rules apply to the computer center.

9. In a couple of lessons, students must save their work. Always give students a name for the saved file and have them add their initials. For example, you may ask students to save a file as **story.their initials**.

10. If parent volunteers or upper-grade students are available, it may be helpful to use them as *computer buddies* for the first few weeks. These helpers can help students get accustomed to the computer software and hardware. *Computer buddies* can also help manage the center rotation if you are using the computer as a learning center.

Computer Center Rules

1. Always type your name on your work.

2. Leave the computer ready for the next person.

3. As soon as your computer time is finished, move to the next activity.

4. Leave the computer area as neat (or neater) than you found it.

reproducible

The best way to introduce a piece of software to students is to demonstrate it. If you have access to a large-screen projection device, you can project what you are doing on your computer onto a movie screen. Or, you may have access to a device which projects what you are doing on your computer onto a television. If you do not have a projection device, show students how to use software in small group sessions at the computer.

Once students have been introduced to the software, allow them time at the computer center to play and become familiar with the tools. If you do not allow exploration time, students will have a difficult time focusing on the activities they are to complete because they will spend time experimenting with the tools. After students have had at least one or two center sessions where they are allowed to explore the software, they will be ready to complete the activities included in this book.

To begin an introduction to new software, open the program using the icon on the computer desktop. Students should be familiar with software icons so they will know what to open. Remind students that to open a program, they need to double-click on the icon.

Once the program is open, show students the opening screen so they are aware of all the options. If they are to work with a specific option, emphasize it.

Once you have been through all the tools, clearly explain what you will want students to do at the computer. Remember to keep it simple and experimental for the first couple of projects. This will be the time for students to explore and experiment. After a few "play" sessions, you can assign a more substantive project. Show students how to save and print their work. Always give them a file name to save it as to make it easy to find their files in the future. Finally, students must know how to quit the program. Students should always quit or exit the program before they leave the computer.

 FS123298 Making the Most of the One-Computer Classroom © Copyright Frank Schaffer Publications, Inc.

If you assign projects that must be completed during scheduled time at the computer, then it is important to use an accountability and assessment system. Two commonly used formats are the checklist and the rubric.

If your primary interest is that students complete the work, a checklist may be all you need.

A checklist form is provided on page 16. Add student names and your list of projects to the form. Tracking is done by checking the appropriate box. The checking can be done by the students themselves, by you, by other students, or by classroom volunteers.

If you are interested in evaluating the work, a rubric will work better for you. A rubric is a qualitative assessment of a piece of work. The work is evaluated against predetermined criteria outlined in the rubric. Two sample rubrics are provided for you on page 17.

To create your own rubric, think about the goals you have for the project—what do you want students to learn? Decide how many rubric levels will work for you (3, 4, 5, or more). Develop the criteria that will be used for assessment using specific descriptors that rely on objective standards of measurement. Clearly-stated rubrics emphasize the product and do not rely solely on a subjective opinion about the product. A useful and effective discussion can be held with your students if you develop the rubric together, because all of you will understand the basis of assessment if you define it together.

What would be an acceptable project? The minimum standards you would accept will be assigned a rubric value. For the purposes of this description we will say that a project that meets your minimum requirements will have a value of 2. What would you expect a project to look like produced by someone who worked hard and effectively? Assign it a value of 3 and define the standards. What about the project produced by the student who was so excited about the project that the product exceeds anyone's wildest dreams? Assign it a value of 4 and define the standards. Anything less than acceptable would receive a 1. If a student does not do the assignment, a 0 is used.

Remember to review the rubric with students before they engage in the assignment and several times during a long term project.

Sample Checklist

Student	Project									

 FS123298 Making the Most of the One-Computer Classroom © Copyright Frank Schaffer Publications, Inc.

Sample Rubric for Seasonal Pictures Lesson *(found on pages 59-60, an art activity)*

3 Dynamic composition and use of positive and negative space. Reflects excellent knowledge of computer program and how to manipulate elements of it. Presentation is thought out and details are finished.

2 Composition is visually interesting. Reflects knowledge of computer program and elements of it. Picture is completed, text is present.

1 Insufficient visual elements to get across idea of the season depicted. Reflects lack of knowledge of the computer program. Insufficient text on page.

Note: On some assignments you may wish to have a two tier rubric—one tier that addresses only the content and originality of the project, and a second tier that addresses only the mechanics of the assignment. A scoring example would be a score of 4/1 on a highly creative piece that does not consistently reflect fundamentals of punctuation and capitalization.

Sample Rubric for Colonial Life Activity *(found on page 69, a multimedia activity)*

4 Reflects extensive research and understanding of the issues of life in the colonies. Illustrations are original and clear. Text is original, clear, and mechanically correct. Dynamic interaction between text and illustration on the cards. Reflects excellent knowledge of computer program and how to manipulate elements of it. Exploits computer media to enhance and animate the presentation. Presentation is thought out and details are finished.

3 Reflects research and knowledge of issues of life in the colonies. Text is clear, and mostly mechanically correct. Illustrations are clear. Balanced composition of text and illustration on individual cards. Reflects good understanding of computer program and how to use it. Use of computer media enhances the presentation. Presentation is thought out and most details are finished.

2 Reflects understanding of life in the colonies. Text is clear, and mechanics are consistent. Cards are adequately illustrated. Each card has text and an illustration. Reflects knowledge of the computer program and how to use it. Use of computer technology makes the presentation clearer. Presentation is done according to the outlines of the assignment.

1 Does not reflect understanding of life in the colonies. Text is unclear, mechanics inconsistent or missing. Cards are not adequately illustrated. Cards are missing elements of text or illustration. Reflects unfamiliarity with computer program. Presentation is not enhanced by computer technology, paper would have sufficed. Missing elements of the assignment.

Is the Internet useful for your teaching and learning? How about for your students? Does the Internet have educational value? The answer is yes! If used properly, the Internet can be an incredible resource for your classroom.

The Internet is the world's largest computer network. Actually, it is a network of networks. Businesses, colleges and universities, individuals, governments, not-for-profit organizations, and secondary and elementary schools are all parts of the network. Through the Internet you and your students can retrieve information in many subject areas, post notes on bulletin boards, correspond with pen pals across the world, "talk" instantly to other users on the Net (typed conversations), and even make Web pages.

The Internet was started by the Department of Defense in 1969 as an experiment in reliable networking to link diverse groups receiving military money such as contractors and university researchers. Of fundamental importance was a design feature called *dynamic rerouting*. This means if one computer in the network went down, communication traffic was rerouted automatically to other components of the network. Since the late sixties, the Internet has evolved from the military network to a military and non-military network. It became a supercomputer network under the auspices of the National Science Foundation, and is now run by independent commercial networks connected through regional networks.

The connection to the Internet is made through a modem, a device that enables data to move from one computer to another over telephone lines. If your school or classroom is not wired with telephone lines, you will not be able to use the Internet. If your school or classroom does have telephone lines, you can get your classroom computer on-line.

Most school districts that allow schools to be wired to the Internet have protection programs to prevent students from viewing inappropriate sites. Generally these programs block out any Internet addresses related to entertainment, adult themes, and sports. There is also software available that allows you to download sites and keep them on your hard drive. The software makes students feel as though they are actually on the Internet when, in reality, they are just viewing sites you have chosen for them. This eliminates unsupervised student use of the Internet. Some schools adopt "acceptable use agreements" that state what is acceptable for students to do on the Internet. Usually these agreements are signed by both students and parents.

On the following pages you will find sites that are useful to teachers. Some of the sites can be used with students, but some are just for you. After visiting these sites, you will see the valuable educational uses of the Internet.

Note: Internet sites change rapidly. The sites listed here were current at the time of the preparation of this book. Explore the content of these sites personally before you send your students to them. Things change quickly in cyberspace!

Search Engines

Search engines are sites that help you find information on the Internet. If you are not sure of the address of a site, or if you just want to know what is out there, a search engine is the place to begin.

There are many search engines on the Internet. Here is a list of some of them, current at the time this book was prepared.

http://www.excite.com   http://www.hotbot.com

http://www.infoseek.com   http://www.lycos.com

http://www.metacrawler.com   http://snap.com

http://www.webcrawler.com   http://www.yahoo.com

Among the many resource sites on the Web, there are sites dedicated to helping teachers do their jobs more effectively by providing resource lists and links to other sites. Some include forums where you can read and post lesson plans or comment on material found on the site.

Teacher Resource Sites

AskEric

http://www.askeric.org

AskEric is a personalized service providing educational information that is part of ERIC, a federally funded national information system that provides a variety of services and products on education. If you have a question about an educational issue, or lesson plans to post, Ask Eric.

The Global Schoolhouse

http://www.gsn.org

This is a resource for exciting on-line projects "Linking Kids Around the World!"

The Library of Congress

http://www.lcweb.loc.gov

This site contains resources from the archives of the Library of Congress, including a learning page for educators.

Teacher2Teacher

http://www.forum.swarthmore.edu/t2t

Resources about teaching mathematics and the ways children learn math.

Teachers Helping Teachers

http://www.pacificnet.net/~mandel

This site is an excellent source of educational links and lesson plans.

Teachers Helping Teachers

http://gnofn.org/~mldean

Although this site shares a name with the one listed above, this site is a different source of education links and lesson plans with some interesting links to Louisiana sites.

U.S. Department of Education

http://www.ed.gov

Language Arts Sites

Children's Literature Web Guide

http://www.ucalgary.ca/~dkbrown

The Complete Works of Shakespeare

http://the-tech.mit.edu/Shakespeare

Project Gutenberg

http://www.gutenberg.net

An electronic public library.

Math Sites

Ask Dr. Math

http://forum.swarthmore.edu/dr.math

Rice University Mathematics Department

http://math.rice.edu/

This site has several interesting sections including well-designed lessons in math, some on the cutting edge. In addition, there is a great deal of practical information on how to encourage girls to learn technology and math.

The Geometry Center

http://www.geom.umn.edu

Math Magic

http://forum.swarthmore.edu/mathmagic

Mega Math

http://www.c3.lanl.gov/mega-math

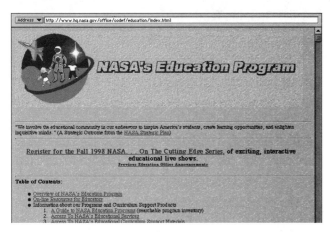

Science Sites

Bill Nye the Science Guy!

http:www.disney.com/DisneyTelevision/BillNye

Discovery Channel's Site for K-12

http://www.school.Discover.com

National Aeronautics and Space Administration

http://www.nasa.gov

Science and Math Education Resources

http://www-hpcc.astro.washington.edu/scied

Sea World/Busch Gardens

http://www.seaworld.org

Here you will find Information about the marine parks, and a tremendous amount of ocean life information and lesson plans for teachers.

Virtual Frog Dissection Kit

http://george.lbl.gov/ITG.hm.pg.docs/dissect

Volcano World

http://volcano.und.nodak.edu

Everything you could want to know about volcanos, with a section for kids, and another section of lesson plans for teachers.

Weather

http://www.weather24.com

The Weather Unit

http://faldo.atmos.uiuc.edu/WEATHER/weather.html

The Yuckiest Place on the Internet

http://www.nj.com/yucky

This site has entertaining science activities for kids.

Social Studies

Discoverer's Web

http://www.win.tue.nl/cs/fm/engles/discovery

This site is a resource guide to information about voyages of discovery and exploration on the web.

History/Social Studies Website for K-12 Teachers

http://www.execpc.com/~dboals

Map Blast!

http://www.mapblast.com

This is a site of interactive detailed maps useful for many educational activities.

Smithsonian Office of Elementary & Secondary Education

http://educate.si.edu

The United Nations

http://www.un.org

The White House

http://www.whitehouse.gov

Women's History Page

http://frank.mtsu.edu/~kmiddlet/history/women.html

There are many great resources for teaching Art, Music, Drama, and Physical Education on the Internet. Also, many Internet providers such as America On-Line and CompuServe offer additional sites only to their subscribers.

Every day there are many more sites on the Internet, and each day new information and addresses are added. Use the information here as a jumping off place, and have fun!

In order to do the activities in this book, students need to know some basic computer operations. Briefly introduce each item on the list below to your students so that they can work independently.

HARDWARE

The Screen

The screen is the face of the monitor. When the computer is turned on, it will give you a list of programs called a menu. Often the screen will have small pictures that accompany a program name. These pictures are called icons.

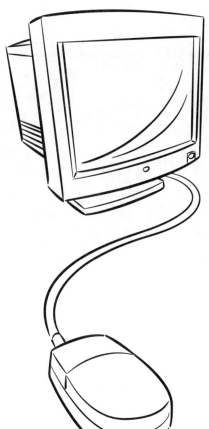

The Mouse

The mouse is the small device attached to the computer that creates an arrow or similar symbol on the screen. This arrow is called a cursor. Moving the mouse to the left moves the cursor on the computer screen to the left; moving the mouse to the right moves the cursor to the right.

To select programs and tools within programs, move the cursor directly onto the icon or word, and click once.

Double-clicking the mouse means clicking twice in rapid succession on the mouse button.

The Keyboard

Important keys to know on the keyboard include the return or enter key, the space bar, the shift key, and the delete or backspace key.

- **Return or Enter key**: moves the cursor to the next line (like the carriage return on a typewriter)

- **Space Bar**: makes a space (like the space bar on a typewriter)

- **Shift Key**: selects a second function for the key (such as capital letters or a symbol)

- **Delete or Backspace Key**: is used for backspacing and/or correcting errors

PRINTING

In the programs referenced in this book, select the *File* menu and then click on *Print*.

Kid Pix Studio and Kid Pix Studio Deluxe

When you open the *Kid Pix Studio* or *Kid Pix Studio Deluxe* program you have several options to choose from. Students should select the Kid Pix option in order to work with the paint tools. The screen opens to a blank white square with a tool bar to the left and a graphic menu bar running horizontally below the blank page.

The *Kid Pix Studio* or *Kid Pix Studio Deluxe* tool bar is what students use to select the tools they need. Below is an explanation of the tools.

The wacky pencil tool is used to draw pictures using free-form lines.

The line tool is also used to draw pictures using straight lines.

The shape tools make squares, rectangles, circles, and ovals.

The wacky brush tool makes lines. It can also be used to paint using a pattern.

The paint can colors backgrounds. It is the tip of the paint can that pours the paint. An object must be completely closed before painting it or the paint will "spill" onto the entire page.

The eraser tool erases either part of a drawing or the whole screen. When this tool is selected, options for erasing appear at the bottom of the screen.

The alphabet text tool allows students to "stamp" letters onto a page. There are options for changing the colors of the letters.

The keyboard tool is used to type text onto the page. Options for different fonts appear at the bottom of the page.

The rubber stamp tool is used to add stamps onto the page. There are several stamp sets available for students to use. They can change the stamp set by clicking on the *Goodies* menu and then selecting *Pick a Stamp Set*. From there, they can select any stamp set they want.

The electric mixer is used to transform a drawing. This is a fun way to add special effects to a drawing. The moving van is used to move part of the drawing. The eyedropper allows the user to "grab" a color used in a picture. The color you click on with the eyedropper will automatically appear in the current color box of the color palette. The last tool in the tool palette is the "Undo" guy. When a mistake is made drawing a picture, the Undo guy can be used to undo the last action.

The color palette is used to change colors of some of the paint tools. Students can select from the colors displayed, or use the arrow keys at the bottom of the color palette to view more color selections.

If you would like to turn off the sound of the tools, this can be done by clicking on the *Toolbox* menu and clicking on *Tool Sounds*. To turn the sound back on, simply click on *Tool Sounds* again.

Pick a ColorMe is located in the *Goodies* menu. This option contains a selection of blackline drawings to color using the paint can tool and color palette.

Another option in *Kid Pix Studio* or *Kid Pix Studio Deluxe* allows students to record their voices reading stories they have written with a microphone accessory. Students click on the *Goodies* menu and then select *Record a Sound*. To record their voices, students click on *Record* and then speak clearly into the microphone. Many Macintosh computers have a built-in microphone. When students are finished recording, they click *Stop*. To save sound to a picture, click on *Save*. To hear the recording, click on *Play*.

The most important thing to remember is to allow students time to explore the program and play with the features. This will make them confident and excited about working with the software.

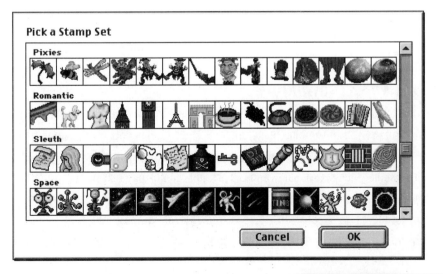

ClarisWorks

When you open the *ClarisWorks* program, you are prompted to select among six options. For the activities in this book, students will select the *Painting* option, the *Drawing* option, the *Word Processing* option, or the *Spreadsheet* option.

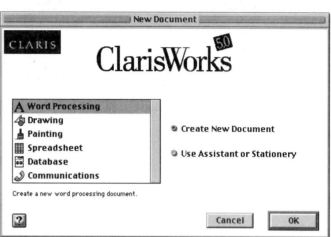

ClarisWorks Painting

When you open *ClarisWorks Painting* you see a white page with a tool palette to the left of the screen. You can paint and add text to the page.

Use the *ClarisWorks* tool palette to select tools. The letter *A* tool is the text tool which must be selected in order to type text. To use it, click on the tool and then click on the screen and start typing.

The painting tools include the paint brush, paint can, spray can, and pencil. Once a paint tool is selected, you can change the color by selecting a new color from the color palette toward the bottom of the tool palette. There are other options available such as changing the gradient or the pattern. When coloring with the paint can, it is the tip of the paint can that pours the paint.

Use the eraser tool to erase mistakes.

The rectangle shape tool makes squares and rectangles. The oval shape tool makes circles and ovals.

The line tool makes straight lines. To change the thickness of the line, use the options at the bottom of the tool palette.

Text can be formatted within the painting option. When formatting text, students change the font, style, and size of the text. Once they have selected the text tool and clicked inside the screen, menu options appear which allow students to format the text in a number of ways.

ClarisWorks Drawing

ClarisWorks Drawing uses many of the same tools as *ClarisWorks Painting*. This powerful option allows you to combine many different kinds of elements on the same page. A drawing document can include objects that you create, select, modify, and move. It can include spreadsheets, text, paint, and clip art. You can link one text frame to another so that text flows from one frame to another. It has a visible grid that can make it easier for some students to create same-size increments on graphs. The tool palette for *ClarisWorks Drawing* is similar to, although smaller than, the *Painting* tools. The

ClarisWorks Help describes the difference between drawing and painting as the difference between making a collage (arranging and layering pieces) and creating a watercolor (adding and blending color and textures). We do not include any activities specifically for *ClarisWorks Drawing* in this book, but some of the activities can be easily accomplished with it, such as drawing bar graphs.

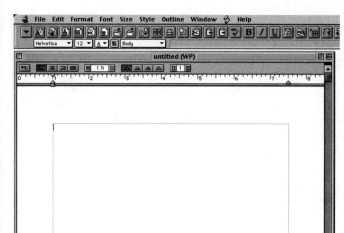

ClarisWorks Word Processing

The *Word Processing* screen looks like a white page with a tool bar across the top. You add words to the page with the keyboard. Graphics cannot be created in this mode, although they can be imported to the screen.

Several activities in this book require text formatting. To change the font, highlight the text you want to change, click on the *Font* menu and then select from any of the fonts listed. The size of the font can be changed by using the *Size* menu. Students can make text bold, italic, or underlined by using the *Style* menu.

To add a graphic, click on the *File* menu and select *Library.* A list of options will appear. Choose a topic and a list of graphics will appear. Select a graphic and click *Use.* The graphic can be moved by clicking on it and moving it while holding down the mouse button. To make the graphic smaller or larger, click on the small box in the right-hand bottom corner and drag. To keep the picture from distorting while you change the size, hold down the shift key while resizing.

ClarisWorks Spreadsheet

When you open the Spreadsheet application you will see a tool bar and a lot of small boxes.

A spreadsheet is used to chart, organize, and analyze information. Data arranged in a spreadsheet can be converted into bar graphs or pie charts by the click of a button in the tool bar. A spreadsheet is made up of rows and columns. Rows are horizontal and numbered along the left side. Columns are vertical and labeled across the top with letters. Each rectangle within the spreadsheet is called a cell. Each cell contains words, numbers, or formulas. Each cell has a name. For example, C2 is where Column C, Row 2 intersect.

Spreadsheets can also have headers (titles). To create a header, click on the *Format* menu and select *Insert Header.* Then type the header for the spreadsheet.

To enter data or a formula, you click inside the appropriate cell and start typing. What is typed appears in the entry bar. When the ✔ is clicked, the entry appears in the cell.

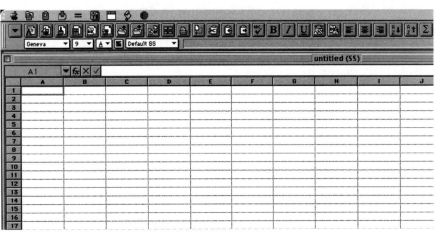

Clicking the *x* cancels the entry. You can also hit return or enter to place the entry in the cell.

Formulas help you make calculations easily and quickly. Formulas always begin with the equal sign (=), followed by the computation to be performed. The following symbols are used: + (addition), – (subtraction), * (multiplication), / (division).

Examples: =4+2   means 4 + 2

              =4–2   means 4 – 2

              =4*2   means 4 x 2

              =4/2   means 4 ÷ 2

When you choose a cell and type a formula in it the cell is programmed by that formula. The formula is visible on the entry bar, but the answer to the formula is visible in the cell. Formulas can include numbers, computation symbols, and other cell names.

The lessons in this book will familiarize students with spreadsheets and give them opportunities to experiment with formulas and other kinds of cell data.

 FS123298 Making the Most of the One-Computer Classroom © Copyright Frank Schaffer Publications, Inc.

HyperStudio

HyperStudio is a multimedia presentation authoring tool. Many of its features work like a painting program such as the painting option in *ClarisWorks.* Like *Kid Pix Studio* or *Kid Pix Studio Deluxe, HyperStudio* can be used to create linear slide shows. It can also be used to create multimedia presentations with alternate sequences (nonlinear).

A *HyperStudio* multimedia presentation is made up of individual "cards." Each screen is a card. Two or more cards are referred to as a stack. When students first open *HyperStudio,* they click on *New Stack* in order to begin working. If they want to view a stack they have already saved, they will need to click on *Open Stack.*

The *Tools* menu contains tools similar to the *ClarisWorks* tool palette. The *Tools* menu in *HyperStudio* can be moved to the side of the screen for easy access. To do this, simply click on the *Tools* menu and drag it to the side of the page. Notice the tools at the bottom of the tools menu. The *Tools* menu includes the paint brush, spray can, paint can, eraser, line tool, pencil, shape tools, and text tool. These tools do the same things they do in other paint programs. To change the colors of the tools, click on the *Colors* menu.

Cards and Stacks

A *HyperStudio* multimedia presentation is made up of individual cards. Each screen is essentially a card. When the student creates two or more cards, it is referred to as a *stack.* In some of the lessons in this book, students create only one card. Other lessons require students to create a stack.

When you first open *HyperStudio*, click on *New Stack* in order to create a new file. To view a stack you have made and saved previously, click on *Open Stack.*

Tools

The tool palette in *HyperStudio* does not automatically appear on the screen. It is retrieved by clicking on the *Tools* menu and dragging it to the side of the page. The tools are similar to those used in other painting programs—the paintbrush, spray can, paint can, eraser, line tool, pencil, shape tools, and text tool (*T*). The colors of the tools are changed by clicking on the *Colors* menu.

The tools at the top of the tool palette are for editing. The *B* edit tool edits any buttons that have been created on a card. (Buttons are used for adding sounds, graphics, and special effects.) The *G* edit tool edits graphics. The megaphone edits sound. The *T* edit tool edits text. The arrow selects objects that you want to move or change. The hand tool is used for clicking on buttons so that you can move around within a stack.

Adding Text

You can add text directly onto the card using the text tool. If the text tool is used to type in text, the text is essentially "painted" onto the card and cannot be changed unless the eraser tool is used to erase the entire text. You can also add text using a *text object*. A text object is a box, or frame, that holds text in place. The text inside this box can be edited with the *T* edit tool.

To add a text object (box or frame), click on the *Objects* menu and select *Add a Text Object*. A box appears on the card. This "text box" will hold the text you want to place on the card. To resize the box, move the cursor onto the frame until an arrow appears; move the arrow to change the box to the desired size. To move the box, click on it and drag it into position.

To format the text appearance, click anywhere on the screen. A dialog box appears and you will see a highlighted box. This box lets you type in a name for the text box that you will create. To pick a color for the text and one for the background, click on the colors in the designated boxes at the left of the screen.

To format the text, click on *Style*. Another dialog box appears, allowing you to choose a font, style, size, and alignment for the text. Once you make your selections, click *OK* on all the dialog boxes. You can then start typing the text.

Working With Buttons

To link individual cards to create a multimedia presentation, you need to add buttons. Buttons are designated by words and/or graphics.

Adding Buttons

To add a button, click on the *Objects* menu and select *Add a Button*. A dialog box appears. First choose a shape for the button. Then in the *Name* box, type the text that you want to see on your button.

Adding Graphics to Buttons

Add a graphic to a button by clicking on *Icons* or *Show Icon*. A screen appears with icons on it. Click on the icon you want and then click *OK*.

Adding Color

Next, use the color palette at the side of the screen to select the color you want for the words on the button. Select a different color for the background. Click *OK*, and the button appears on the card. To move the button into place, click on it and drag it.

Objects	
Add a Button...	⌘B
Add a Graphic Object...	⌘G
Add a Text Object...	**⌘T**
Hypertext Links...	⌘L
Bring Closer	⌘+
Send Farther	⌘-
About this Card...	
About this Stack...	

Objects	
Add a Button...	⌘B
Add a Graphic Object...	⌘G
Add a Text Object...	⌘T
Hypertext Links...	⌘L
Bring Closer	⌘+
Send Farther	⌘-
About this Card...	
About this Stack...	

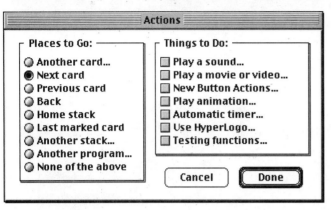

Adding Actions

Next, click anywhere on the screen to add the button "actions." A dialog box appears labeled *Actions*. Actions are sounds and/or special effects that occur when the button is pressed.

First look at the *Places to Go* box and select *Next card*. This indicates that you are setting up the button on your card so that once you press it, the next card in your stack will appear. When you select *Next card*, a box labeled *Transitions* appears. A transition is a special effect that takes place when you press the button and move from one card to the next. You will see a list of transitions. Choose one and then click *OK* to return to the dialog box labeled *Actions*.

Sounds are added to your button by clicking on *Play a Sound* in the *Things to Do* box. A dialog box appears with a list of sounds and a picture of a tape recorder. Select one of the sounds on the list. If you want to preview the sound, click *Play* on the tape recorder. Then click *OK* to get back to the *Actions* dialog box. Then click *Done*.

Adding Graphics to Cards

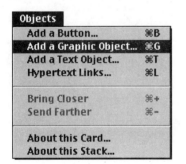

You can add graphics to cards by going to the *Objects* menu and selecting *Add a Graphic Object*. You will see a list of labels indicating the types of graphics that are available. Click on one of the labels. You will then see an arrangement of graphics associated with that label. Click on one of the selection tools at the top left-hand corner of the screen; this lets you ring the graphic you want. Then click *OK*. You will see the graphic on your card. Move the graphic to where you want it. Then click anywhere on the screen. A dialog box appears. The options in this box let you add sound and other special effects to your graphic.

Give students plenty of time to explore the program. As they play with the many fun features of *HyperStudio* and work through the activities in this book, they will become excited about creating colorful multimedia presentations on their own.

Primary Word Processing Activities

Type the Letters

Provide a template of the alphabet in capital letters for your pre-literate students. Students match the capital letters on the keyboard with the capital letters on the template and type each letter in alphabetical order. Note: choose a font for the template that resembles the letters on the keyboard.

First Words Practice

Give students a list of basic words to type into the computer. This simple activity helps students practice letter recognition as they type the words on the computer keyboard. It also helps them practice spelling and reading. After students print out the list of words, ask them to read the words to a friend.

Write a Story

Students write a simple story and type it into the computer. If students are ready, show them how to use spell check. They can illustrate their stories with computer or freehand drawings.

One day a butterfly named Sara went to the river. She went to the river to go to a party.

Type Your Name

Young students can practice spelling and writing their names at the computer. They type their names using the computer keyboard. Show students how to use the *Shift* key in order to make a capital letter.

Alphabetize Words

Give students a list of words to alphabetize. Have students type them into the computer in the proper order. Use spelling words or words related to a theme you are teaching.

What If? Stories

Give students a situation and then ask, *What would happen if . . .* Examples: *What if you woke up and you were suddenly an adult? What if you woke up and you had duck feet?* You can challenge students to come up with their own *what if* topics to exchange with partners.

Copy Student Dictation

Expand the student literacy process. Have a student "oral author" dictate a story. Then word process the story. Provide the word-processed version of the dictation to the "oral author" to copy and practice reading aloud. Students will be learning about spaces between words, correct punctuation (and how to find it on the keyboard), and know and be interested in the material they are copying. For students in the early reading stages, this is a powerful learning tool.

What's the Word?

Give students a series of picture cards and have them type words for the pictures into the computer. You could use theme-related pictures for this activity.

Long and Short Vowels

Students practice their formatting skills in the word processing program by typing a series of words you provide and making words with long vowels bold and words with short vowels italicized.

Contractions

Give students a list of contractions and ask them to type in the two words that make up each contraction. You can also do this activity in reverse by giving students two words and asking them to type the contraction. Or, challenge them by combining both options.

Writing Your Way

Have students write and type a new chapter for a book they are reading. You may want to have each student write a new ending to a book the class has read together or for a read-aloud book you have shared. Then have fun comparing the endings.

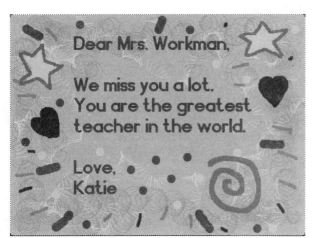

Be a Friend

Have students write friendly letters to people they know. Review the friendly-letter format, which can include a heading, greeting, body, closing, and signature. Post a sample letter at the computer for students to follow.

Abbreviation Practice

Give students a list of abbreviations and ask them to type the word for each abbreviation. A list of basic abbreviations is provided below.

St.	Sat.	yr.	min.	Dr.	Sun.	yd.	gal.
in.	hr.	ft.	Tues.	Rd.	P.O.	Fri.	cm

Illustration Exchange

Students draw or paint a picture which they then exchange with another student. The second student writes a story based on the picture. An extension of this project is to have the illustrator provide copies of the picture to several different students who each write a story about the picture. Compare the stories and discuss point of view and how perceptions are similar and different from person to person.

The Never-Ending Story

Create a story document on the computer. Begin a story as a class and enter the opening paragraphs in the document. Afterwards, a student adds the next section or adventure. Then other students take turns adding to the story to create a class chapter book.

Theme Words

Give students a theme to ponder. Ask them to type in as many words as they can think of that relate to that theme. Use their lists to develop a class chart of theme words.

Parent Awareness

Keep parents informed of classroom activities by having students use the computer to type a few sentences about what they are learning in school that week. They can also write a few sentences announcing the study of a new theme or write a note requesting materials they should bring in from home for a project. Give them as many opportunities as possible to show parents how they are using technology — and keep parents informed in the process.

Dictated Stories

Allowing kindergartners to dictate stories, as a parent types them, adds a dimension to story dictation. Print the stories and allow students to read them to the class, or you can read them out loud.

Writing About Me

Ask students to write about themselves and type the information into the computer. After students have all completed their biographies, allow them to share them with the class. Some sample prompts are:

- My family consists of...

- What I like to do most is...

- When I am older...

- What makes me really happy is...

If I Were in Charge

Read some of the poems in *If I Were in Charge of the World and Other Worries* by Judith Viorst (Aladdin, 1981) to students. Have them consider what they would do if they were in charge of the world. Then, have them write about it using the computer. Projects can be printed and made into a class book for all to enjoy.

Rhyme Time

Give students a list of words for which there are many rhyming words. Ask them to choose any of the words from the list and type in as many rhyming words as they can think of. Students can print their lists so you can create a rhyming wall using all the rhyming words the class came up with.

Upper-Grade Word Processing Activities

Opposites Attract

Give students a list of words and have them type in the antonyms. As an extension, they can type in synonyms. Below is a list of words to use.

in	right	noisy
up	dark	day
big	lost	open

My Teacher Is Missing!

Read the story *Miss Nelson Is Missing!* by Harry Allard (Houghton Mifflin, 1985) to students. Ask them to write about what it would be like if Miss Viola Swamp came to their class to teach for a week. How would the students react? What kind of homework would she give? What would happen when their teacher finally returned to the class?

Story Starters

Create a set of cards that include settings for stories such as a castle, a deserted island, a school playground, or a campground by the river. Place these setting cards inside a hat. Then, have each student select a card from the hat and create a story based on that setting. Students type the stories into the computer and print them. Stories can be shared with other students in the class or placed in a class book for all to enjoy.

Fun With Rocks

Read the story *Everybody Needs a Rock* by Byrd Baylor (C. Scribner Sons Young, 1974) to the class. Using the computer, students develop their own list of rules for finding the perfect rock and print them. Then, take a nature walk as a class and try to find perfect rocks according to their rules.

Sequence Strips

Have students type the events of a story in correct sequence into the computer creating several blank lines between each event. Then, they print out **two copies** of the page and cut apart the sentence strips from one of the copies. Sentence strips are placed in an envelope with the name of the story written on the outside. The second copy of the events is placed inside the envelope to be used as an answer key. These could be placed at a center or used as a free-time activity.

Personal Journals

Students type an entry into their electronic personal journals each week. At the end of the month, their journal is printed and placed inside a personal journal folder decorated by each student. This would be a good time to introduce students to the importance of the privacy of computer files.

Fairy Tale Twist

Students love fairy tale twists. Read a few samples to students prior to the activity. Suggested books include *The True Story of the Three Little Pigs* by Jon Scieszka (Viking, 1989), *The Frog Prince Continued* by Jon Scieszka (Viking, 1991), *The Paper Bag Princess* by Robert N. Munsch (Firefly Books Ltd., 1980), and *Little Red Riding Hood and The Wolf's Tale* by Della Rowland (Carol Publishing Group, 1991). After reading some samples, have students write their own fairy tale twists and type them into the computer. Putting these together makes a fabulous class book.

Business Letters

Students write business letters to companies expressing their thoughts and opinions about the products and services provided by the company. Brainstorm ideas with the whole class to decide what to write about.

Part II

Have students write a sequel to a story they have read. Tell them to keep some of the main characters and add some new ones. Decide together whether the location of the story can be changed in the sequel.

Acrostic Poems

Acrostic poems are easy to write because they do not have to rhyme. Writing personal acrostics are even easier. Students type their names into the computer vertically. Then, they choose a word that describes them for each letter of their names. Format the first letter of each word so that it stands out. They can make the font size larger and perhaps bold as well. An example follows.

> **J**oyful
>
> **O**bedient
>
> **H**onest
>
> **N**ice

Kid Pix Studio or Kid Pix Studio Deluxe Activities

Story and Picture

Have students use the paint tools in *Kid Pix Studio* or *Kid Pix Studio Deluxe* to draw pictures for their own stories. If it is difficult for students to draw a picture and write a story on the same page, have them draw a picture in one session, and write the story in a second session.

Picture Dictionary

As students encounter unfamiliar words and take the time to look them up, they can develop their own picture dictionaries. Using *Kid Pix Studio* or *Kid Pix Studio Deluxe*, students can draw a picture for a word and then type in a definition. These printed pages become a personal picture dictionary for each student.

My Likes and Dislikes

Students stamp things they like on the right side of the screen and things they don't like on the left. These pictures can be printed and discussed with partners or as a class.

Create an Ad

Bring in some print ads from magazines. Students analyze them to determine what the ads are trying to sell and what text or graphics are being used to try to sell it. Then students design new ads for a product. Remind them to use descriptive language and words that will convince someone to buy the product or service.

Write a Poem

Suggest students create light, pastel background pictures with the paint tools. Discuss different types of poems such as haiku, cinquain, couplet, free verse and so on. Have students write a poem at the computer. Then they write their poems by typing the text right over the picture using a dark color for the text so it will show up.

ColorMe

Kid Pix Studio or *Kid Pix Studio Deluxe* has a wonderful option called "ColorMe." This option allows a student to choose a picture to color. The blackline art can be very detailed, so be sure students know they will have to exercise patience. Also, remind students that it is the tip of the paint can that pours the paint. They should place the tip inside the lines to pour paint in each section of the picture. After they have finished painting, they write a story about the picture they chose.

Software: *Kid Pix Studio* or *Kid Pix Studio Deluxe* (Brøderbund)

Technology Prerequisites: Students must be able to use the alphabet text tool and the stamp tool.

Content Skills: letter recognition, recognizing initial sounds, following directions

Technology Skills: using the keyboard, the text tool, and the stamp tool

Literature: *The Icky Bug Alphabet Book* by Jerry Pallotta (Charlesbridge, 1986), *Wildflower ABC* by Diane Pomeroy (Harcourt Brace, & Co., 1997), *Animalia* by Graeme Base (Harry N. Abrams, Inc., 1986)

Lesson Objective

Students create alphabet books using the letters and stamps in *Kid Pix Studio* or *Kid Pix Studio Deluxe*. The projects can be individual alphabet books or a class alphabet book.

Lesson Plan

1. Read several alphabet books with students. You may want to read some of the unusual alphabet books listed above. Tell students that they will create their own alphabet books using the computer.

2. Explain to students that they will use *Kid Pix Studio* or *Kid Pix Studio Deluxe* to make their alphabet books. They will type the letter onto the page. They should also type their names at the bottom of the page. Then, they will stamp pictures onto the page that begin with the sound of that letter. (Remember that *c* and *s* can have the same sound, as can *g* and *j*.)

3. To change stamp sets students click on the *Goodies* menu and select *Pick a Stamp Set*. They will find a variety of stamp sets and stamps.

4. Tell students that they need to have at least ten stamps for each letter.

5. Remind students that they will print their work.

6. Students should also be reminded to quit or exit the program when they are finished so that the computer is ready for the next student.

7. You may want to review the steps on the activity card with students so that they can work independently at the computer.

8. Have students make nice covers for their alphabet books.

Assessment Criteria

1. Student has typed the correct letter on the page.

2. Student has chosen ten stamps to represent the letter sound.

3. Student has chosen stamps that correctly represent the letter sound.

Make an Alphabet Book

1. Open the *Kid Pix Studio* or *Kid Pix Studio Deluxe* program.

2. Select the alphabet text tool. Type the letter or sound you will get pictures for.

3. Type your name at the bottom of the page.

4. Look for stamps of pictures that begin with the sound on your page. Stamp them onto your picture.

5. If you need different stamps, click on the *Goodies* menu. Select *Pick a Stamp Set*.

6. You need ten stamps on your page.

7. Print.

8. Quit or exit the program.

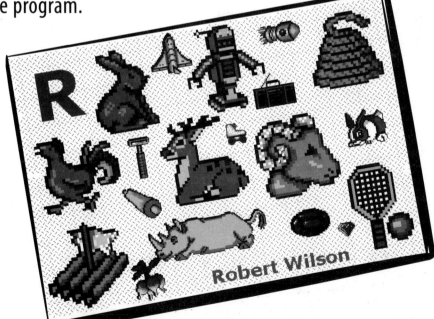

reproducible

Software: *Kid Pix Studio* or *Kid Pix Studio Deluxe* (Brøderbund) or *ClarisWorks* Painting Application (Apple)

Technology Prerequisites: Students must be able to use the keyboard text tool in *Kid Pix Studio* or *Kid Pix Studio Deluxe* or the text tool in *ClarisWorks*.

Content Skills: spelling, critical thinking, following directions

Technology Skills: keyboarding, using text tool

Lesson Objective

Students love to solve puzzles. In this activity, students type the answers to a series of questions. Then, they will use the first letter of each answer to discover a mystery word. Students practice spelling and keyboarding skills as well as critical thinking skills as they put the letters together to solve the mystery.

Lesson Plan

1. Explain to students that they will be detectives trying to solve a mystery.

2. Tell students that they should use the keyboard text tool in *Kid Pix Studio* or *Kid Pix Studio Deluxe* or the text tool in *ClarisWorks* to type the answer to each question found on the activity card.

3. They can solve the mystery by joining the first letter of each of the answers they have already typed.

4. Students should add the mystery word as well as their first names to the bottom of the page. Then they should print their work.

5. Students should also be reminded to quit or exit the program when they are finished so that the computer is ready for the next student.

6. You may want to review the steps on the activity card with students so that they can work independently at the computer.

Assessment Criteria

1. Student has followed directions.

2. Student has answered each question correctly.

3. Student has solved the mystery.

Find the Mystery Word

1. Open the *Kid Pix Studio* or *Kid Pix Studio Deluxe* or *ClarisWorks* program. If you are using *ClarisWorks*, select the *Painting* option.

2. Select the keyboard text tool in *Kid Pix Studio* or *Kid Pix Studio Deluxe* or the letter *A* text tool in *ClarisWorks*.

3. Type the answers to the questions below.

   What is the name of a creature that lives in the ocean and has eight arms?

   What is the name of a sea creature that is small, flat, and has pinchers?

   What is the name of a slithery creature that looks like a snake but lives in water?

   What is the name of a sea creature that looks like a colorful flower?

   What does a fisherman use to scoop fish out of the water after they are caught?

4. Type the first letter from each of the above answers to discover the mystery word.
   Your clue is: it is wet and salty.

5. Type your first name at the bottom of the page.

6. Print.

7. Quit or exit the program.

reproducible

Software: *Kid Pix Studio* or *Kid Pix Studio Deluxe* (Brøderbund)

Technology Prerequisites: Students must be able to use the keyboard text tool and the stamp tool.

Content Skills: spelling, creative writing, capitalization and punctuation, following directions

Technology Skills: keyboarding, using the stamp tool, using the text tool

Literature: *Spot's Walk in the Woods* by Eric Hill (Puffin, 1993)

Lesson Objective

In this activity, students write a rebus story using the stamps in *Kid Pix Studio* or *Kid Pix Studio Deluxe*. In order to keep this activity to 20 minutes, you may wish to have students work out their stories before they use the computer. In this case you will want to provide a list of stamps available. In the *Kid Pix Studio* or *Kid Pix Studio Deluxe User's Manual* that accompanies the program, you will find pictures of the Rubber Stamps in the Stamp Sets.

Lesson Plan

1. Explain to students that they will be using *Kid Pix Studio* or *Kid Pix Studio Deluxe* to write a rebus story. You may wish to read the literature selection suggested above to ensure that all students know what a rebus story is.

2. After reading the story, ask students to write their own rebus stories using the list of stamps as a reference. Tell them to plan to use these stamps/words in their rebus stories.

3. Be sure that students know how to use the keyboard tool and the stamp tool. They should type their stories using the keyboard tool, leaving a blank space where they are going to use stamps instead of words. When done with the text, the students stamp the symbols into their stories. Note: In *Kid Pix Studio Deluxe,* you can move from the text tool to the stamp tool and then back to the text tool without having to leave blank spaces.

4. Remind students to check spelling and to use proper capitalization and punctuation.

5. Students should type their names at the bottom of the page, then print their work.

6. Remind students to quit or exit the program when they are finished so that the computer is ready for the next student.

7. You may want to review the steps on the activity card with students so that they can work independently at the computer.

Assessment Criteria

1. Student created a rebus story.

2. Student used correct punctuation and capitalization.

3. Student placed stamps correctly.

Write a Rebus Story

1. Open the *Kid Pix Studio* or *Kid Pix Studio Deluxe* program.

2. Select the typewriter text tool.
   Type the words to your story. Leave blanks in the places where you will use a stamp instead of a word. Note: In *Kid Pix Studio Deluxe*, add stamps to your story as you are writing.

3. Check your spelling, capitalization, and punctuation.

4. Type your first name at the bottom of the page.

5. Select the stamp tool.
   Add the stamps to the correct places in your rebus story.

6. Print.

7. Quit or exit the program.

One ![stamp] ![stamp] after a hard day of ![stamp] ![stamp],

Jane, ![stamp], went to sleep under her ![stamp]

next to the ![stamp]. She used her ![stamp] for a

pillow. She had a strange dream.

reproducible

Primary Painting Activities

Experiment with Overlapping Shapes

Students use the shape tools to make circles, ovals, squares, and rectangles. Then, they can use the line tool to make other shapes such as triangles and diamonds. When students have printed their pictures, discuss how overlapping makes some things appear closer than others.

Know Your Numbers

To help students become more familiar with numbers and to practice number recognition, have them type in the numbers 1 through 10 in the correct order.

Beginning Fractions

Have students draw circles and squares using the shape tools. Then, they use the line tool to divide the shapes into halves. Next, they draw two rectangles and divide them into thirds and fourths.

Telling Time

Students can use the circle tool to make clock faces and the line tool to create the hands of the clocks. They print these out to share with partners who determine what time is indicated on each of the clocks.

Number Patterns

Give students a list of number patterns to complete. Explain that students should type the missing numbers into the pattern. This will help them practice number identification and also keyboarding skills. They can use the numbers at the top of the keyboard, or you may want to introduce them to the number pad if you have one on your classroom keyboard. Some number pattern samples are:

2	4	6	_____
3	6	_____	12
4	8	12	_____

Circular Flash Cards

Have students use the oval shape tool to make large circles. Inside each circle, they type a math problem. Students print their pages, cut out the circles, and write the answer on the back of each card. Partners take turns choosing a circle and answering the math problem on it.

Upper-Grade Painting Activities

Design a Maze

Students love to do mazes. They are wonderful for visual-spatial intelligence. Now students can design their own mazes using the computer. Using the line tool, students can create mazes to challenge their friends. One way to approach creating the maze is to draw the correct route from the beginning to the end first, label the starting point and ending point, and then add lots of dead ends. When students are finished, they can print out the mazes and share them with friends.

More Fraction Projects

Students use the rectangle and oval tools to make several circles, squares, and rectangles. Then have students divide the shapes into halves, thirds, and fourths, and color sections to represent a fraction. For example, students divide a rectangle into fourths, and shade three-fourths of the rectangle by using the paint can to pour paint into the sections to equal that fraction.

Measuring Lines

Have students use the line tool to make five lines of different length on the screen. Then have students print out these lines and use their rulers to measure the length of each one. They can trade with a partner to check their answers.

Writing Numbers

Give students a series of numbers written with words. For example, ask them to type the digits for three hundred seventy-six in the computer. You can also do this activity in reverse by giving a series of digits (like 376) and asking students to type the words for the number.

Create a Tangram

Have students use the line tool to create their own tangrams. They can print and cut out the pictures and use them to make tangram picture cards.

Round 'Em Up

Give students a series of numbers to round up to the nearest ten or hundred. The correct answers can be entered into the computer using the text tool.

Kid Pix Studio or Kid Pix Studio Deluxe Activities

Multiplication Practice with Stamp

Have students use the stamps to create multiplication problems. They can create and answer their own problems or they can swap with a friend and answer the friend's problems.

Match a Pattern

Create a pattern using the stamps and print it for students to review. Then have students match the pattern using the stamps. Or, students can create patterns on their own and swap with partners. The next time the partner is at the computer, he or she must try to duplicate the pattern.

flowers

trees

fruits

people

Make a Number Line

Have students make number lines that they can keep at their desks. They should type in the numbers 1 through 10, leaving space for stamps. Under each number they should stamp the number of items representing that number. These can be printed out and taped to the desks or around the room for students to refer to and practice with.

Develop a Calendar

Students can use *Kid Pix Studio* or *Kid Pix Studio Deluxe* to make their own calendars adding stamps to show holidays, special events, and reminders for classroom projects and activities.

Write Word Problems

Students often have the most trouble with word problems. By writing some themselves, they may gain a better idea of how to solve them. Students can write word problems using the keyboard text tool. Then they can use the paint tools to draw a picture representing each story problem. For example, the problem may be "There are three apple trees with four apples on each. How many apples in all?" Students will draw three apple trees with four apples in each as a picture representing the word problem. They can give their word problems to other students to solve.

Simple Bar Graphs

Stamps from the *Kid Pix Studio* or *Kid Pix Studio Deluxe* collections can be used to make simple bar graphs. One example is a class food survey. Students identify their favorite fruit from the following choices: apple, pineapple, pear or strawberry. Each of these fruits is represented by a stamp in the collections. Have students make the bar graph by creating a row or column using one repetition of the appropriate food stamp to represent each student who chose that fruit as a favorite.

Making Graphs with Painting Software

Spider Size

Students make a bar graph showing the length of spiders using the line tool. For this activity, students make enough lines for ten different types of spiders along the horizontal side. Along the vertical side they label the graph beginning with 0 millimeters and going up by increments of 10 millimeters until they get to 100 millimeters. Here is information needed to complete the graph.

tarantula = 90 mm

spitting spider = 8 mm

American house spider = 8 mm

black widow = 32 mm

garden spider = 11 mm

trap door spider = 30 mm

funnel web mygalomorph = 50 mm

purse web spider = 30 mm

dwarf spider = 2 mm

nephila = 25 mm

Ancestry Bar Graph

This bar graph compares the population of various ethnic groups in the U.S. To make the graph, students should label the ethnic groups along the vertical side. Then they should label the horizontal side numerically, in increments of 10 million, starting with 10 million and ending with 50 million. Use an almanac to supplement the following data.

English = 49,598,035

Native American = 6,715,819

Mexican = 7,692,619

Irish = 40,165,702

African-American = 20,964,729

French = 12,892,246

Ocean Bar Graph

This graph compares the average depths of the world's oceans. Students label the vertical edge of the graph with the names of the oceans. Then they can label the horizontal side numerically in increments of 500 beginning with 500 meters and ending with 4500.

Arctic Ocean = 1,200 m

Southern Ocean = 3,730 m

Pacific Ocean = 4,150 m

Atlantic Ocean = 3,300 m

Indian Ocean = 3,900 m

Energy Pie Chart

Students can use the line tool to create pie charts to show where our energy comes from.

petroleum oil = 43%

coal = 24%

nuclear energy = 7%

hydroelectric energy = 4%

natural gas = 22%

Math Computer Activities (cont.)

Spreadsheet Activities

Note: You might enjoy experimenting with a feature of the *ClarisWorks* spreadsheet option. Simple bar graphs and pie charts can be automatically generated by the program. Select the information to be graphed and click on the appropriate button at the extreme right end of the tool bar.

Drive Around the Planets

Provide students with the information below regarding the circumference of each planet. First, students create the header "Driving Around the Planets." The first column of the spreadsheet (column A) should list the names of each of the planets. Column B should list the circumference of each planet in miles. In Column C, enter the rate of speed students will be driving—the number 50. Then, students enter a formula in the fourth column (column D). For example, if Pluto is the planet listed in A1, then the formula entered in D1 would be: =B1/C1. The equals sign indicates to the computer that this is a formula. The B stands for column B and the number 1 stands for the first row in that column. The slash is the standard sign for division. The C1 stands for the number of miles per hour students will be driving around the planet.

Mercury = 9,517 miles	Venus = 23,616 miles	Earth = 24,888 miles
Mars = 13,260 miles	Jupiter = 278,976 miles	Saturn = 235,180 miles
Uranus = 99,736 miles	Neptune = 96,712 miles	Pluto = 4,490 miles

Once students have entered all the figures and formulas, have them change the driving speed in Column C to 75. Then, let them watch how that changes the figures in Column D. Because the formula is already programmed, changing the driving speed, instructs the computer to recalculate the figures automatically.

 FS123298 Making the Most of the One-Computer Classroom © Copyright Frank Schaffer Publications, Inc.

Parachute Physics

Students investigate parachutes, including the factors that would influence the rate at which a parachute will fall such as wind, length of its lines, fabrication material, weight and balance, size, and shape. They test how the size of the parachute affects the rate at which it falls. In small groups students construct three parachutes of the same material in three different sizes. They collect the following data about each parachute: measurements of the parachute and the area and the time the parachute used to hit the ground in three separate trials. On a spreadsheet, students enter the identifying information and the data they collected. Use the formula function to figure average flight durations for each parachute (the sum of the three flight times/3 or the number of test flights made if more or less than 3).

Counting Calories

First, students create the header "Calorie Intake." In column A of the spreadsheet, students enter the foods listed below. In column B, students list the calories for each item as indicated. Then provide students with a list of portions of each food item which students should enter in column C. In the fourth column (column D), they enter this formula: (=B1*C1). The equals sign indicates to the computer that it will be a formula. The B1 indicates the calories, the asterisk indicates to multiply, and the C1 indicates the portion. The computer will calculate the caloric value. Now give students a second list of portions. They should make the quantity changes in column C and watch how the changes affect the totals in column D.

banana = 100	apple = 80	cupcake = 130
tuna = 170	milk = 150	yogurt = 230
fried egg = 85	chicken drumstick = 90	

Calorie Intake

	A	B	C	D
1	banana	100	1	100
2	apple	80	2	160
3	cupcake	130	1	130
4	tuna	170	2	340
5	milk	150	3	450
6	yogurt	230	2	460
7	fried egg	85	2	170
8	chicken drumstick	90	2	180
9				

Software: *Kid Pix Studio* or *Kid Pix Studio Deluxe* (Brøderbund)

Technology Prerequisites: Students must be able to use the keyboard text tool and the stamp tool.

Content Skills: recognizing patterns, following directions

Technology Skills: using the stamp tool, using the text tool

Literature: *Brown Bear, Brown Bear, What Do You See?* by Bill Martin Jr. (Holt, 1983), *Over the Steamy Swamp* by Paul Geraghty (Harcourt, Brace, Jovanovich, 1988), *The Napping House* by Audrey Wood (Harcourt, Brace, Jovanovich, 1984)

Lesson Objective

Students explore creating patterns using the variety of stamps in *Kid Pix Studio* or *Kid Pix Studio Deluxe*. You may want to extend the activity by having students swap patterns with partners and then having the partners try to guess what the pattern is and what stamps would come next in the pattern.

Lesson Plan

1. Read some of the pattern books suggested above to students. Discuss how patterns can be seen or heard. Have students practice making visual patterns using manipulatives to refresh their skills before they go to the computer to make their own patterns.

2. Explain that students will use the stamps in *Kid Pix Studio* or *Kid Pix Studio Deluxe* to create visual patterns on their own. They can use any stamp set or sets they would like. Have them make at least three different patterns.

3. If students want to change stamp sets, they can do this by clicking on the *Goodies* menu and then selecting *Pick a Stamp Set*. There are a variety of stamp sets to choose from.

4. Have students use the text tool to add their names to the bottom of the page, and then have them print out their work.

5. Students should also be reminded to quit or exit the program when they are finished so that the computer is ready for the next student.

6. You may want to review the steps on the activity card with students so that they can work independently at the computer.

Assessment Criteria

1. Student created three patterns.

2. Each of the patterns was different from the other two.

3. Student used the stamp and text tools properly.

Stamp a Pattern

1. Open the *Kid Pix Studio* or *Kid Pix Studio Deluxe* program.

2. Select the stamp tool and make a pattern.

3. Use the stamp tool to make two more patterns.

4. Select the text tool and type in your name.

5. Print.

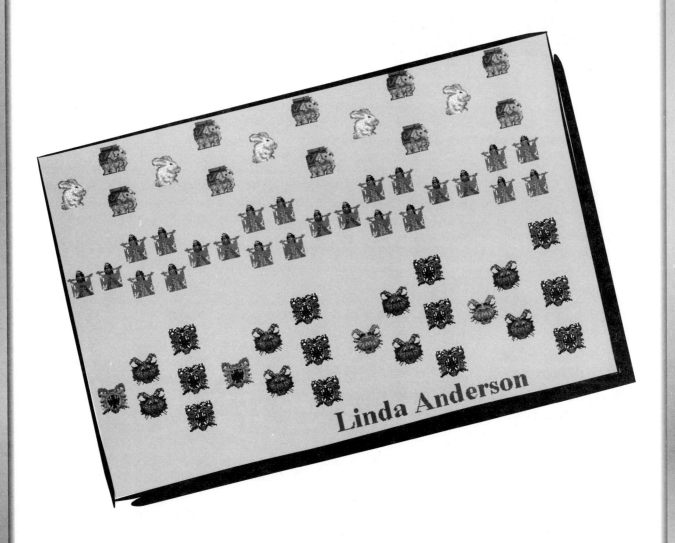

reproducible

Software: *ClarisWorks* Painting Application (Apple)

Technology Prerequisites: Students must be able to use the line tool, rectangle tool, paint can, color palette, and text tool.

Content Skills: graphing, following directions

Technology Skills: using the line tool, paint can, color palette, and text tool

Lesson Objective

In this lesson, students conduct a survey and then create a graph using the painting option in *ClarisWorks*. Students need to have all their data prior to going to the computer to work. Each student should poll as many people as they can including people outside of the classroom.

Lesson Plan

1. Have students poll people to find out when their birthdays are and keep track of this data. Encourage students to include classmates, teachers, and family members as part of their survey. The more data they collect, the more interesting the graph. You may want to require a minimum sample.

2. Explain to students that after they have collected their data, they will create a graph on the computer. They should use the line tool to draw the graph. The x-axis will represent the months and the y-axis the numbers of people who have birthdays in a given month. Explain to students that if they hold down the shift key while using the line tool, they can draw easily.

3. Tell students to use the text tool to type the names of the months below the horizontal axis, and numbers representing people on the vertical axis next to the horizontal increment lines.

4. Students use the text tool to type their names on their pages.

5. Students use the rectangle tool to draw bars that represent the data they collected. Then they color the bars with the paint can. To make a colorful graph, students change colors for each bar with the color palette.

6. Students print their graphs then quit or exit the program when they are finished.

7. You may want to review the steps on the activity card with students so that they can work independently at the computer.

Assessment Criteria

1. Student collected the data.

2. Student created the graph lines correctly.

3. Student labeled the graph correctly.

4. Student converted raw data to an accurate bar graph.

5. Student used the tools correctly.

Make a Birthday Bar Graph

1. Open the *ClarisWorks* program. Select the *Painting* option.

2. Select the line tool and draw the graph. Months will be labeled along the x-axis (horizontal line), and quantities on the y-axis (vertical line). Add horizontal lines to mark the location of the number. Note: if you hold the shift key down while you draw a line, you will get a straight line.

3. Select the text tool and type the labels for the graph.

4. Type your name at the bottom of the page.

5. Select the rectangle tool to add the bars to your graph.

6. Select the paint can and color the bars. Use the color palette to change colors.

7. Print.

8. Quit or exit the program.

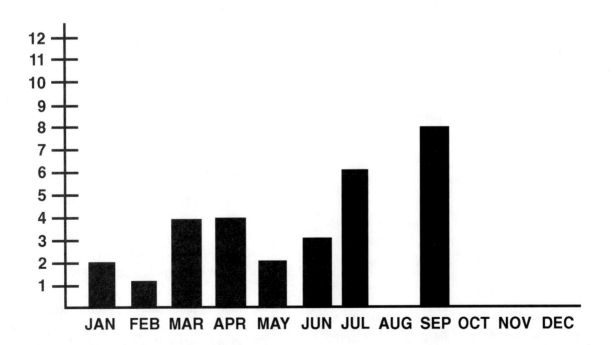

reproducible

Sports Spreadsheet

Software: *ClarisWorks* Spreadsheet Application (Apple)

Technology Prerequisites: Students must be able to enter formulas and insert headers on spreadsheets.

Content Skills: division, decimals, algebra, sports percentages

Technology Skills: spreadsheet formulas, spreadsheet formats

Lesson Objective

This lesson gives students practice in using spreadsheets to calculate sports percentages. The percentages will reflect the number of games won by basketball teams.

Lesson Plan

1. Tell students that keeping track of wins and losses helps determine which team has performed the best in a playing season and that they will be creating a spreadsheet in *ClarisWorks* to see how team standings are calculated in sports.

2. Students select the *Spreadsheet* option and insert a header by clicking on the *Format* menu and selecting *Insert Header*. They title their spreadsheet *Basketball Winnings,* hit the return key, and type their name on the second line. Tell students that they will be comparing the statistics of six fictitious basketball teams.

3. In sports, wins and losses are used to calculate a team's winning percentage. A winning percentage indicates the number of games a team can be expected to win if it plays 1,000 games. To determine the winning percentage, the number of wins is divided by the total number of games played (the number of wins and the number of losses). For example, a team plays 12 games, winning 9. Divide 9 by 12, which gives a percentage of .750. If the team played 1,000 games, it would be expected to win 750. The winning percentage is written with three numbers to the right of a decimal.

4. Students enter these column headings: *Teams* for Column A, *Wins* for Column B, *Losses* for Column C, and *Percentages* for Column D. Next, have them enter the names of the six teams (Dragons, Stars, Titans, Jaguars, Comets, Falcons), beginning with A2 and ending with

A7. Once students have entered the team names, they follow the directions on the activity card and input the wins and losses in Columns B and C.

6. The spreadsheet must be set up to calculate the winning percentage. (In *ClarisWorks*, you must indicate how you want the answer to a division problem to be displayed.) First, students highlight the cells in Column D, from D2 to D7. Then they click on the *Format* menu and select *Number*. A dialog box labeled *Format Number, Date, and Time* will appear. Students will select *Fixed* and click on *3* in the part labeled *Precision*. This will show the winning percentage correctly.

7. Next, students enter the formula (number of wins divided by the number of games). To do this, they click on D2 and enter **=B2/(B2+C2)**. (Remind the class that formulas begin with an equal sign and that the division sign is indicated by a slash.) The answer that appears in D2 will be the winning percentage for the Dragons (the team listed in A2). Students continue clicking on each of the remaining cells in Column D and typing the appropriate formula to find the rest of the winning percentages. For example, for D3, they enter **=B3/(B3+C3)**.

8. Let students add other teams and statistics to the page and calculate winning percentages for them.

9. Tell students to print their spreadsheet and to exit the program when they are finished so that the computer is ready for the next student.

10. For a follow-up activity, let students look in the newspaper and compare the statistics of their favorite sports teams.

Assessment Criteria

The student set up the spreadsheet correctly.

The student entered data in the correct cells.

The student entered the formulas correctly.

Sports Spreadsheet

1. Open the *ClarisWorks* program. Select the *Spreadsheet* option.

2. Insert the header. To do this, click on the *Format* menu and select *Insert Header*. Type **Basketball Winnings**. Hit the return key and type your name on the second line.

3. Type the headings for four columns. Type **Teams** in A1, **Wins** in B1, **Losses** C1, and **Percentages** in D1.

4. Enter the team names in Column A. Begin with A2 and end with A7.

   Dragons

   Stars

   Titans

   Jaguars

   Comets

   Falcons

5. Enter the wins for each team in Column B. Begin with B2 and end with B7. Enter the losses for each team in Column C. Begin with C2 and end with C7.

	Wins	Losses
Dragons	35	25
Stars	40	28
Titans	42	23
Jaguars	48	17
Comets	28	38
Falcons	47	19

Sports Spreadsheet (cont.)

6. Now you are ready to set up Column D to calculate the teams' winning percentages. First highlight D2 through D8. Click on the *Format* menu and select *Number*. A dialog box will appear. Under the options for *Number*, click on *Fixed*. For *Precision*, click on *3*. Now when you calculate the percentages, you will get three figures to the right of the decimal point (such as 0.583).

7. Click on D2. Enter the formula for calculating the winning percentage for the Dragons:

$$=B2/(B2+C2)$$

The formula shows that the Dragons' number of wins is to be divided by the total number of games played (the number of wins and the number of losses). After you enter the formula, the winning percentage appears in D2.

8. Enter the formulas that will get you the winning percentages for the remaining teams. Remember to begin each formula with an equal sign (=) and to use a slash (/) for division.

9. Add other teams to your spreadsheet. Make up their wins and losses, and calculate their winning percentages.

10. Print your spreadsheet.

11. Quit or exit the program.

Basketball Winnings
Shannon Lo-O'Malley

	A	B	C	D	E	F
1	Teams	Wins	Losses	Percentages		
2	Dragons	35	25	0.583		
3	Stars	40	28			
4	Titans	42	23			
5	Jaguars	48	17			
6	Comets	28	38			
7	Falcons	47	19			
8						
9						
10						
11						
12						

FS123298 Making the Most of the One-Computer Classroom © Copyright Frank Schaffer Publications, Inc.

reproducible

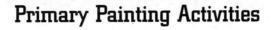

Primary Painting Activities

Over the Rainbow

Show students pictures of rainbows and discuss the order of the colors in the rainbow. Starting at the top, the correct order of a rainbow is red, orange, yellow, green, blue, and purple. Have students use the line tool and paint can to draw and color a rainbow. Remind students that the individual color arches in the rainbow must be closed shapes so that the paint can doesn't spill paint all over the picture.

Insect Drawing

Show students a variety of insects and talk about the parts of an insect body. Many insects have three parts to their bodies: a head, an abdomen, and a thorax. After students have examined a variety of insects, have each student draw an insect of their choice on the computer and label its parts using the text tool.

Match a Color

You will need to prepare this activity in advance so that students will have something to match. Use the square shape tool to make five or six squares. Color each a different color. Then, print the page. Give this page to students and tell them to draw the squares and match the colors you used on your sample. This will help students practice their colors.

Sea Creature Mobile

Allow students to draw and print several computer pictures of sea creatures or ocean plants. These pictures can be cut out and assembled into a mobile. Students should punch a hole in each picture and then feed string through the hole. Then attach the string to a coat hanger. When the mobiles are finished, display them.

My Important Pet

Have students draw pictures of pets they have or would like to have. Have them write one or two sentences about what they need to do in order to properly care for the pets. These can be printed and displayed on a bulletin board about caring for and being responsible for pets.

Weather Picture

Discuss different types of weather with students. Students draw pictures showing one kind of weather.

Paint the Planets

Have students use the shape tools and line tool to draw all of the planets. Provide any reference materials they need in order to be prepared with sufficient background knowledge to complete this project.

Upper-Grade Painting Activities

The Human Body

Students can use the paint program to draw an outline of the human body. They can use the text tool to label the basic parts of the human body such as arms, legs, heart, stomach, head, ears, eyes, and so on. If you have done a unit on the human body and students have sufficient background knowledge, you can have them label some of the internal organs such as the liver and kidneys. If you have been studying the human body, you may also want to have students write a fact or two at the bottom of the page based on what they have learned.

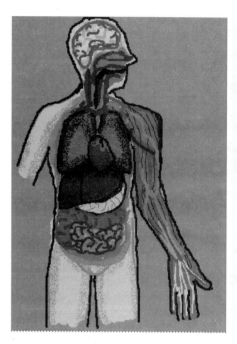

Rain Forest Picture

Students create pictures that represent the rain forest. A couple of good titles to help build students' background knowledge are *The Great Kapok Tree* by Lynne Cherry (Harcourt, Brace, Jovanovich, 1990) and *Welcome to the Green House* by Jane Yolen (Putnam, 1993).

Life Cycles

Often students study the life cycle of an animal. Instead of having them draw the life cycle on paper to show what they have learned, have them draw the life cycle using the computer. You may want to have students use the line tool to divide the page into an appropriate number of sections for the stages in the life cycle of the animal they have chosen. Then, in each section, students should draw a stage of that animal's life cycle.

Building Circuits

After doing a hands-on project in which students build and test a circuit, have them draw their circuit using the computer. They should label each part of the circuit and write an explanation of how to build and test a circuit at the bottom of the page.

Vertebrates vs. Invertebrates

Have students begin this project by drawing a line down the center of the page using the line tool. They can use the text tool to make a list of animals that are vertebrates and those that are invertebrates. Have them draw a picture of any one of the animals.

Moon Phases

Students can use the circle tool to make four full moon shapes. They can use the pencil tool and paint can to shade in a section of the full moon to indicate each of its four phases. Students should also use the text tool to label the four phases.

Kid Pix Studio or Kid Pix Studio Deluxe Activities

Magnetic Attraction

Students can use the stamps in *Kid Pix Studio* or *Kid Pix Studio Deluxe* to show what they know about magnetism. Begin this activity with a hands-on demonstration of a magnet. Have several objects available for students to look at. Then have them guess which items will stick to the magnet. After they have completed this hands-on activity, they can go to the computer for follow-up. Have them choose stamps of objects that a magnet would attract and stamp them onto the page. They can print these pages and compare them to a friend's pages to see if they both got the same answers. Any items in question should be tested with the real magnet.

Classifying Animals

There are many animal stamps in the *Kid Pix Studio* or *Kid Pix Studio Deluxe* stamp sets. They can be used for many kinds of classification activities depending on the level of your students. Animals can be sorted in groupings such as: how many legs they have; vertebrate or invertebrate; mammal, amphibian, reptile, bird, fish; habitat (terrestrial or aquatic); how they move; warm- or cold-blooded; or, mythical or real.

HyperStudio Activities

Food Group Multimedia Presentation

Students develop a food group multimedia presentation. They should have a title card for their presentations that includes their name. Students should create a card for each food group, with either drawn or clip-art examples from that food group. They can use the text tool to list other items that belong to that food group. You may want to challenge them to list the number of servings from that food group they should try to eat each day.

Poisoning Prevention Presentation

Students develop multimedia presentations about poisons and safety around poisonous substances to present to younger students. Presentations can include recognizing poisons, safety precautions, and what to do in case of poisoning or suspected poisoning.

Space – The Final Frontier

Students develop multimedia presentations about the history of space explorations that can include the history of technology and the history of the people behind it such as space explorers who have never left earth (like Copernicus or Carl Sagan) and those who have (like Sally Ride and John Glenn). Extensions of this project can be done which include presentations about what might be found on other planets in our solar system, or in other galaxies, or the birth of a star.

Senses Multimedia Presentation

Students build a multimedia presentation to show what they know about the five senses. They should all begin their presentations with a title card that shows the title and their names. They should develop at least one card for each sense using text, drawing pictures or importing graphics or clip art to represent that sense. *HyperStudio* has many built-in graphics that students can use.

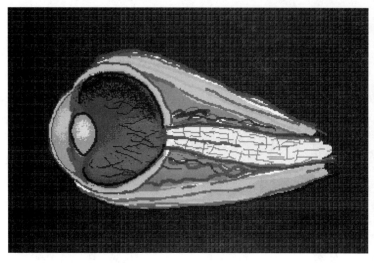

The Importance of Climate

Climate is the sum of all the weather events in an area over an extended period of time. There are 12 types of climate: 1) tropical wet, 2) tropical wet and dry, 3) highlands, 4) deserts, 5) steppe, 6) subtropical dry summer, 7) subtropical moist, 8) oceanic moist, 9) continental moist, 10) subarctic, 11) polar, and 12) icecap. Climate affects how people live. Students can work in groups to focus on one climate type and aspects of daily life affected by it such as, clothing, food, housing, transportation, animal life, and plant life. Small group presentations can be linked to create one large multimedia presentation on the importance of climate.

Necessity, the Mother of Invention

Students choose an important scientific discovery or invention. They create multimedia presentations about the history of the discovery or invention and the person who made the discovery or created invention. What was life like before the discovery? How did the discovery change people's lives?

The Science Game

Students create their own games in the subject matter you are studying. The game "board" is a series of cards. Students can create question, answer, action, penalty, and reward cards that move a player through the stacks of the game. Each card has one or more choices of action that can be taken based on the criteria of that card. The possibilities are endless.

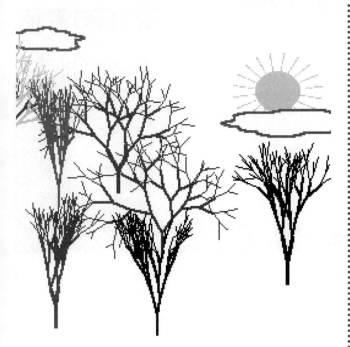

Software: *Kid Pix Studio* or *Kid Pix Studio Deluxe* (Brøderbund) or *ClarisWorks* Painting Application (Apple)

Technology Prerequisites: Students must be able to use the text tool, pencil tool, paint brush, and paint can, and be able to change the colors of the paint tools by using the color palette.

Content Skills: four seasons, following directions

Technology Skills: using the pencil tool, paint brush, paint can, color palette, and text tool

Literature: *Winter Across America* by Seymour Simon (Hyperion, 1994), *Spring Across America* by Seymour Simon (Hyperion, 1996), *Changes* by Marjorie N. Allen and Shelley Rotner (Aladdin, 1991)

Lesson Objective

It is fun to learn about the different seasons, particularly if you live in an area where the seasonal change is not very dramatic. You may want to build background knowledge for students in this activity. Keep in mind that, depending on where you live, some of your students may never have touched snow. You may elect to have students draw pictures of what a season is like in your area.

1. Discuss the four seasons with students. If students are not familiar with a cold winter (including snow), you may want to spend time building background knowledge. The books suggested above, particularly *Winter Across America*, are good resources for this activity.

2. Explain to students that they will draw pictures of a season of their choice. Be sure to tell students of anything specific you want them to include in their drawings.

3. Encourage students to use all the paint tools to draw their pictures. They should use the color palette to change the colors of the paint tools. Then they should use the text tool to label the season.

4. Remind students to type their first names at the bottom of the page when they are finished and to print out their work.

5. Students should also be reminded to quit or exit the program when they are finished so that the computer is ready for the next student.

6. You may want to review the steps on the activity card with students so that they can work independently at the computer.

Assessment Criteria

1. The student drew an appropriate picture.

2. The student used the paint tools correctly.

3. The student used the text tool correctly.

Seasonal Pictures

1. Open the *Kid Pix Studio* or *Kid Pix Studio Deluxe* or *ClarisWorks* program. If you are using *ClarisWorks*, select the *Painting* option.

2. Use the paint tools to draw a picture of the season of your choice.

3. Make your picture colorful by using the color palette to change the colors of the paint tools.

4. Use the text tool to label your picture with the name of the season.

5. Type your name at the bottom of the page.

6. Print.

7. Quit or exit the program.

FS123298 Making the Most of the One-Computer Classroom © Copyright Frank Schaffer Publications, Inc.

reproducible

Software: *Kid Pix Studio* or *Kid Pix Studio Deluxe* (Brøderbund)

Technology Prerequisites: Students must be able to use the paint can tool and be able to change the color of the paint can. They should also be able to use the typewriter text tool in *Kid Pix Studio* or *Kid Pix Studio Deluxe*.

Content Skills: learning about nature, following directions

Technology Skills: using the paint tool, color palette, and text tool

Literature: *Water Dance* by Thomas Locker (Harcourt, Brace, Jovanovich, 1997), *Grassroots* by Carl Sandburg (Harcourt, Brace, Jovanovich, 1998), *Here Is the Southwestern Desert* by Madeleine Dunphy (Hyperion, 1995), *Rocky Mountain Seasons* by Diane L. Burns (Macmillan, 1993)

Lesson Objective

Kid Pix Studio or *Kid Pix Studio Deluxe* has a wonderful feature called *ColorMe*. It includes drawings that students can color by using the color palette and the paint can. To find this feature, click on the *Goodies* menu and select *Pick a ColorMe*. For this lesson, students can choose any picture in the *Nature* category and then color it according to their individual preferences. You could display the printed pictures on a bulletin board display celebrating nature.

Lesson Plan

1. Read some of the suggested nature books to students. Discuss the beauty of nature. Ask them to describe some of the colors of nature they saw in the books. Now, tell students that they are going to color a nature picture that has been already drawn in the computer.

2. Explain the *ColorMe* feature in *Kid Pix Studio*. Invite students to choose any nature picture they want. They can use the paint can to paint the picture with the colors of their choice. Remind students that it is the tip of the paint can that pours the paint, so they should place the tip very carefully.

3. Remind students to use the color palette to change the color of the paint can.

4. Ask students to use the typewriter text tool to write their names on the white space around their pictures. After they have added their names, they should print out the pictures.

5. Students should also be reminded to quit or exit the program when they are finished so that the computer is ready for the next student.

6. You may want to review the steps on the activity card with students so that they can work independently at the computer.

Assessment Criteria

1. Student used paint can correctly.

2. Student used typewriter text tool correctly.

"ColorMe" Nature

1. Open the *Kid Pix Studio* or *Kid Pix Studio Deluxe* program.

2. Click on the *Goodies* menu and choose *Pick a ColorMe*.

3. Choose the *Nature* category and then choose any picture you would like to color.

4. Select the paint can to color in the picture. Make it colorful by selecting different colors from the color palette!

5. Select the typewriter text tool to type your name on the white space.

6. Print.

7. Quit or exit the program.

FS123298 Making the Most of the One-Computer Classroom © Copyright Frank Schaffer Publications, Inc.

reproducible

Software: *ClarisWorks* Spreadsheet Application (Apple)

Technology Prerequisites: Students must be able to enter spreadsheet formulas and insert headers.

Content Skills: multiplication, algebra, mass, gravity

Technology Skills: spreadsheet formulas, headers

Lesson Objective

Students learn that the force of gravity is different on Earth than it is on the moon or the other planets, and that this difference affects the weight of an object. Students use the spreadsheet in *ClarisWorks* to chart how an object's weight varies, depending on its location in the solar system.

Lesson Plan

1. Show your students pictures of astronauts on the moon. Tell them that even though the astronauts had to wear heavy equipment, they were able to walk easily on the moon because they were not as heavy as they were on Earth. Explain that the force of gravity on the Earth is six times greater than on the moon; this means that the astronauts weighed only one-sixth of what they weighed on Earth. Explain that the force of gravity is weaker on the moon because the moon's mass (the amount of matter) is much smaller than Earth's.

2. Students create a spreadsheet to compare weights on Earth with weights on the moon and planets. They select the spreadsheet option in *ClarisWorks*.

3. Next, students insert the header by clicking on the *Format* menu and selecting *Insert Header*. They type *Weights in Outer Space* and then add their names on the second line.

4. Once students have created the header, they enter the names of the moon and planets in Column A, from A1 to A10. They enter 100 (weight in pounds) in Column B, from B1 to B10.

5. In Column C, students enter numbers that compare the force of gravity on the moon and the planets to that on Earth. For example, they will enter .17 for the moon, which means that if the force of gravity on Earth were represented by the number 1, then the force of gravity on the moon would be one-sixth of 1. The numbers to be keyed-in are listed on the activity card.

6. In Column D, students enter the formulas for computing relative weights. In D1, they enter the formula for determining weight on the moon: **=B1*C1**. Once the formula is entered, the relative weight is automatically calculated in D1.

7. Students enter the appropriate formulas in the remaining cells in Column D. Once all the formulas have been entered, students will see that something weighing 100 pounds on Earth has varying weights in outer space.

8. Students print the spreadsheet. Then have them change the weight Column B to 120 to see that the spreadsheet automatically adjusts the weights in Column D.

9. Let the students experiment using other numbers for the weights. Ask them how much they would weigh on the moon or the other planets.

10. When students have finished experimenting, let them print their final spreadsheet.

11. Remind students to quit or exit the program when they are finished.

Assessment Criteria

1. The student entered data on the spreadsheet correctly.

2. The student entered the formulas correctly.

3. The student experimented with the weights.

Planetary Weight

1. Open the *ClarisWorks* program. Select the *Spreadsheet* option.

2. Insert the header. To do this, click on the *Format* menu and select *Insert Header*. Type **Comparing Weights**. Then hit the return key and type your name on the second line.

3. Enter the following names in Column A:

   Earth's Moon
   Mercury
   Venus
   Earth
   Mars
   Jupiter
   Saturn
   Uranus
   Neptune
   Pluto

4. Enter **100** in Column B for rows 1 to 10. The 100 represents a weight of 100 pounds.

5. Enter the following numbers in Column C. The numbers show how the moon and planets compare in mass to the Earth.

	Earth's Moon	.17
	Mercury	.38
	Venus	.90
	Earth	1.00
	Mars	.38
	Jupiter	2.87
	Saturn	1.32
	Uranus	.93
	Neptune	1.23
	Pluto	.06

	A	B	C	D
1	Earth's Moon	100	0.17	
2	Mercury	100	0.38	
3	Venus	100	0.9	
4	Earth	100	1	
5	Mars	100	0.38	
6	Jupiter	100	2.87	
7	Saturn	100	1.32	
8	Uranus	100	0.93	
9	Neptune	100	1.23	
10	Pluto	100	0.06	
11				

FS123298 Making the Most of the One-Computer Classroom © Copyright Frank Schaffer Publications, Inc.

reproducible

Planetary Weight (cont.)

6. Enter the formulas to find out how much a 100-pound weight would weigh on the moon and the planets. First enter the formula for the moon. Click on D1. Type the following formula:

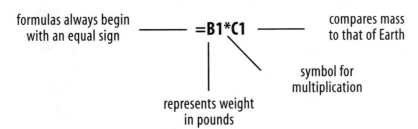

formulas always begin with an equal sign ——— **=B1*C1** ——— compares mass to that of Earth

represents weight in pounds

symbol for multiplication

7. Once you enter the formula for D1, the weight appears in the cell. It shows how heavy a 100-pound weight would be on the moon.

	A	B	C	D
1	Earth's Moon	100	0.17	17
2	Mercury	100	0.38	
3	Venus	100	0.9	

8. Enter formulas in Column D to show how heavy a 100-pound weight would be on the different planets. Each time you will need to indicate that the weight (the number in Column B) is multiplied by the corresponding number in Column C. For example, D4=B4*C4.

9. Print your spreadsheet.

10. Change 100 pounds to 120 pounds. See how the spreadsheet automatically calculates the new weights in Column D.

11. Change the weight to a different number. What happens in Column D?

12. Print this last spreadsheet.

13. Quit or exit the program.

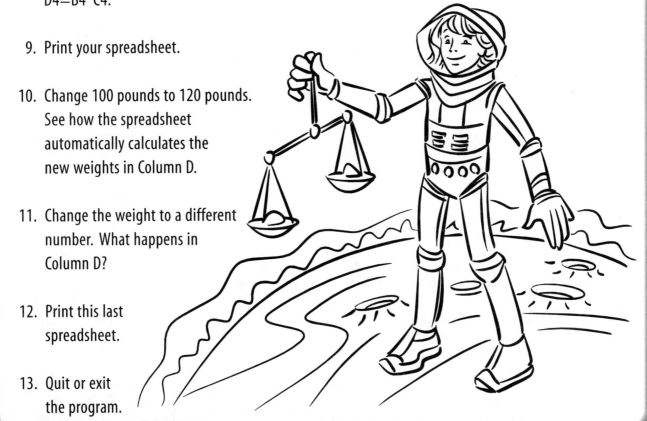

Primary Painting Activities

Look at Me
Students use the paint tools to draw self-portraits. These pictures can be displayed together on a bulletin board celebrating all the different "Me's" in the class.

Transportation Puzzle
Discuss with students different types of transportation. Then challenge them to draw detailed pictures that include a transportation vehicle. Have them print the picture and glue it to tagboard. After the picture has dried, they can cut the picture into puzzle pieces.

My Family
Invite each student to create and color a decorative border on a page using the paint tools. Print the borders. Have students bring a picture of each family member from home that they can glue onto the page. These make an excellent display.

Classroom Quilt
Have each student create an original design that fills the entire screen. Students print their masterpieces. These pictures can be attached to one another to create a classroom quilt of designs. These look fabulous and are fun to display throughout the year.

Totem Poles
Students use the paint tools to create a Native American totem pole. Begin by sharing books that have examples of totem poles. Talk about the symbolism of the totem pole. Ask students to pay close attention to the designs on the totem poles. Brainstorm what computer tools they can use to create similar designs on their totem poles. Student designs can be used as templates for a class totem pole made from ice-cream cartons (available from ice-cream retailers), or other reusable/recyclable items.

Good Citizenship
Students use the paint tools to illustrate one of the behaviors of a good citizen. They use the text tool to write a caption about their drawing. Some ideas include: good citizens pick up litter; good citizens use inside voices while they are inside; good citizens share; good citizens walk quietly in the halls; and so on. Print the signs and display them.

Upper-Grades Painting Activities

Peace on Campus

Discuss the concept of "peace" with students. You may want to read *Peace Begins with You* by Katherine Scholes (Little, Brown, and Company, 1990). Discuss with students how they could promote peace on your campus and between students. Have each student design a peace symbol using the paint tools and then add a sentence or two describing what the symbol means. These can be printed and displayed throughout the school to bring every student's attention to the importance of peace on campus.

Thank You

Discuss different community workers and the importance of their jobs. Have students write a thank-you letter to a community worker of their choice such as school custodian, librarian, bus driver, paramedic, mayor, teacher, firefighter, trash collector, or police officer.

Historical Cinquain

Have students brainstorm different historical figures. Explain that they will use the paint tools to draw one of these historical figures. After students have drawn their pictures, challenge them to write cinquain poems describing the subject. Here is the pattern for a cinquain poem.

noun (the subject)	**Harriet Tubman**
adjective (describing word), adjective (describing word)	**Courageous, resourceful**
verb (action word), verb (action word), verb (action word)	**Leading, enduring, encouraging**
four-word phrase (about the subject)	**Daring rescuer of slaves**
free line (summary)	**Dedicated to freeing an enslaved people.**

Then and Now

Have students draw and print a map of the 13 colonies. Then have them draw and print a map of the same area as it exists now. The maps can be glued alongside each other and used for comparison discussions.

Wanted Poster

Turn this traditional activity into a game. Students use the paint tools to draw a historical "bad guy" and describe this person and his or her nasty deeds under the picture without including the name. These could be printed and displayed. Have a contest to see which student can guess the names of the most people from the posters.

Kid Pix Studio or Kid Pix Studio Deluxe Activities

Holiday Card

Students can use the paint tools and stamps to design and create holiday cards for any special day. You may want them to make holiday cards to give to their parents or friends. Encourage students to make their cards as artistic as possible.

My Favorite Things

Have students use the stamps to show their favorite things. They can also write in this activity. Have them write statements followed by a stamp. For example, they can write "My favorite food is" and then finish the statement with a stamp representing their favorite food. Ask them to include at least five different statements and stamps.

Sun Patterns

Read *Arrow to the Sun* by Gerald McDermott (Viking, 1974) to students. It is a Caldecott-winning adaptation of a Pueblo Indian tale. Have students take a favorite story and make illustrations in the style of Mr. McDermott's drawings.

Postage Stamps

A few times a year, the United States Postal Service issues special stamps honoring people and events such as Elvis Presley and the first person walking on the moon. Challenge students to design new stamps based on people or events that have been in the news lately.

Celebration Picture

Kid Pix Studio or *Kid Pix Studio Deluxe* has a wonderful option called *ColorMe*. One of the choices available is *Celebrations*. Have students click on the *ColorMe* option and select *Celebrations*. A list of options appears. Have students choose any picture to color.

Neighborhood Map

Students can draw maps of their neighborhood using the line tool. Then they can use stamps to show various landmarks within their community. There are many stamps that are appropriate for this activity. Be sure that students know how to change stamp sets. They should use the text tool to label the streets on the neighborhood map.

HyperStudio Activities

Colonial Life

Have students each create a multimedia presentation based on a colony of their choice. The first card should be a title card and include a map of the colony and the name of the colony. The student's name should also appear on this page. Then there should be a card for each of the following topics:

Housing—Draw a typical house.

Clothing—Draw a man or woman wearing typical clothes.

Food—List foods they would have eaten. Draw one of the foods.

Schooling—What was school like for the children?

Fun—What did the colonists do for fun?

Campaign Manager

If there is an upcoming election, have students choose a popular candidate for this project. They can choose an official already in office and complete this project for his or her reelection campaign. Students can create a multimedia presentation to highlight the accomplishments and qualifications for their candidates. Tell them to keep in mind that their goal is to persuade people to vote for their candidates. Students should then display their presentations to the class to inform others about their candidates. You could even hold an election following the presentations to see who was the most convincing.

Time Travel – Local History

Students prepare a multimedia presentation of the history of your community. This can be a group or individual project. Include such topics as regional and local maps, historical maps, historical and current photos of local places of interest (see note), special events in the community, excerpts from journals of local residents of the past and now, and any other interesting information. Consult your local historical society for research resources on your community.

Note: Photos can be scanned in a computer file, and brought into *HyperStudio* on your computer via a computer disc. If your school does not have a scanner, it is possible one of your students does, or you may find a local stationery or business supply store that will provide this service.

Personal Portfolio

Students create personal portfolios to highlight their accomplishments. These multimedia presentations could then be played at an open house event or parent night. Students should begin the project by brainstorming lists of things they can include in their portfolios. They should consider academic achievements, sports awards, things they do that make them special, community service, and work experience (babysitting, gardening, various chores, and so on). Once students have chosen the topics, they can create their presentations. As a twist on this activity for older students, have them create a portfolio to take with them on a job interview. You can provide a job description or it could be for any job students would someday like to have.

Discovery and Exploration

Students create a multimedia presentation about an explorer or explorers that includes biographies, maps, routes, and significant discoveries or outcomes of the exploration. You may want students to research information such as the types of transportation used, what kinds of supplies were brought along, duration of trips, what types of clothing and weapons the explorers had, and how they dealt with any people they met along the way.

The Civil War

Students create a multimedia personal journal of a person living through the Civil War. Presentations can be made from the point of view of a soldier, a woman in a besieged city, a slave, an abolitionist, a prisoner of war, a slave owner — there are no limits to the imagination of your students. Using photos in books as reference, students can draw their own pictures to illustrate the sights that they want the viewer to see.

Personal Time Lines

As a class create a time line of important world events in *HyperStudio*. Then students create personal time lines of their lives that include significant dates and events of their lives by year. They create links from their time lines to the class-generated time line.

Family Trees

This multimedia project encourages students to create as extensive a family tree as they can. Each card can represent a generation, or just one person with links back and forth through time to ancestors, siblings, or offspring. Students go back as far in their family history as they are able. Interesting information to include for each person includes dates of birth and death, significant dates or events in their lives, or any interesting information about him or her.

Software: *Kid Pix Studio* or *Kid Pix Studio Deluxe* (Brøderbund)

Technology Prerequisites: Students must be able to use the line tool and stamp tool, and the typewriter text tool.

Content Skills: learning about transportation, categorizing, following directions

Technology Skills: using the line tool, stamp tool, and text tool

Lesson Objective

Students will use *Kid Pix Studio* or *Kid Pix Studio Deluxe* to share their knowledge of transportation vehicles. Students will divide a page into three section and use stamps to show methods of transportation for air, sea, and land. Students can use the text tool to label the categories on their charts.

Lesson Plan

1. Brainstorm with students the different modes of transportation. Share examples of each of those modes.

2. Explain to students that they will each be making a chart in *Kid Pix Studio* or *Kid Pix Studio Deluxe* to show examples of three modes of transportation: by air, by sea, and by land.

3. Tell students that they should first draw the chart using the line tool. Then they should use the typewriter text tool to label the three parts of the chart.

4. After the chart has been drawn, students can use the *City* stamp set to look for stamps that are examples of modes of transportation.

5. Remind students to put their first names or initials on the charts and then to print out their work.

6. Students should also be reminded to quit or exit the program when they are finished so that the computer is ready for the next student.

7. You may want to review the steps on the activity card with students so that they can work independently at the computer.

Assessment Criteria

1. Student constructed chart correctly.

2. Student accurately categorized the stamps.

3. Student used the typewriter text tool correctly.

Transportation Charts

1. Open the *Kid Pix Studio* or *Kid Pix Studio Deluxe* program.

2. Select the line tool and draw two lines to separate the page into three sections.

3. Select the typewriter text tool and label the chart with: AIR, SEA, and LAND.

4. Then type your name at the bottom of the page.

5. Go to the *Goodies* menu and select *Pick a Stamp Set*.

6. Choose the *City* stamp set.

7. Select the stamp tool and choose stamps that fit into the three categories.

8. Print.

9. Quit or exit the program.

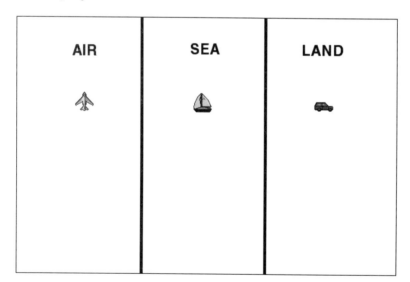

FS123298 Making the Most of the One-Computer Classroom © Copyright Frank Schaffer Publications, Inc.

reproducible

Software: *Kid Pix Studio* or *Kid Pix Studio Deluxe* (Brøderbund) or *ClarisWorks* Painting Application (Apple)

Technology Prerequisites: Students must be able to use the line tool, the paint brush tool, and the typewriter text tool.

Content Skills: Native Americans, following directions

Technology Skills: using the line tool, paint brush tool, and text tool

Lesson Objective

Native Americans often used symbols as substitutes for words. In this lesson, students will create symbols for some common words and then write messages to one another. Students will have to try to decipher the messages they receive based on the symbols. In the column at right are some sample symbols that you may want to share with students in order to help them get started with this activity.

Lesson Plan

1. Discuss the use of symbols by Native Americans. Draw the symbols below on the board. Have students guess what each may be a symbol for.

2. Give students a common word like *school*. Ask them to brainstorm a symbol that could be used as a substitute for the word.

3. Explain to students that they are going to create messages and use symbols for some of the words. They can use some of the symbols you showed them, but they should also create some of their own.

4. Tell students that after they finish their messages, they will all be printed. Then you will give each of them a message from another student to try to decode.

5. Remind students to put their first names or initials on the messages and then to print their work.

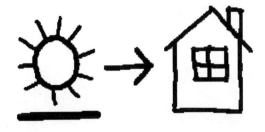

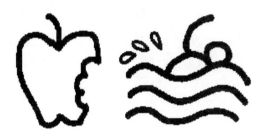

6. Students should also be reminded to quit or exit the program when they are finished so that the computer is ready for the next student.

7. You may want to review the steps on the activity card with students so that they can work independently at the computer.

Assessment Criteria

1. Student created an original message.

2. Student decoded another student's original message.

3. Student used the tools correctly.

Native American Message

1. Open the *Kid Pix Studio* or *Kid Pix Studio Deluxe* or *ClarisWorks* program. If you are using *ClarisWorks*, select the *Painting* option.

2. Select the line tool and paint brush tool to create a message using symbols you create. Make your symbols as identifiable as possible.

3. Select the text tool.

4. Type your name at the bottom of the page.

5. Print.

6. Quit or exit the program.

FS123298 Making the Most of the One-Computer Classroom © Copyright Frank Schaffer Publications, Inc.

reproducible

Software: *HyperStudio* (Roger Wagner Publishing)

Technology Prerequisites: Students must be able to use the text tool, pencil tool, paint brush and paint can, and change colors of the tools using the color palette. Students must also be able to create new cards and text boxes as well as add buttons, button sounds, button transitions, and button text.

Content Skills: learning about states, researching, following directions.

Technology Skills: using the pencil tool, paint brush, paint can, color palette, and text tool; creating new cards, text boxes, new buttons, button sounds, button transitions, and button text

Lesson Objective

In this lesson, each student will research a state and create a multimedia presentation based on the research information. Students can research the information using traditional tools, electronic reference materials, or the Internet. Note that depending on the level of expertise students have with *HyperStudio*, this lesson may take several sessions.

Lesson Plan

1. Ask students if they have ever visited another state. Brainstorm a list of some states students would like to visit or are interested in. Then ask each of them to choose a state for this activity.

2. The presentations should contain at least five cards in the stack, including a title card, map of the state, sites to see, a picture of the state flower and bird, and information on the elected officials of that state.

3. Presentations are enhanced by using the full range of *HyperStudio* tools. The first card is the title card of the presentation and should include a graphic that represents the state and would make someone interested in visiting or finding out more about that state. Remind students that when working in *HyperStudio* they can change the size and shape of the pencil or paint brush. This can be done by clicking on the *Options* menu and then selecting *Line Size* or *Brush Shape*.

4. Students use the text tool to type the name of the state and their own names. Note that when students type onto the background without creating a text box first, the text is "painted" onto the background and cannot be changed.

5. To move from the first to the second card, students will add a button to the card by clicking on the *Objects* menu and select *Add a Button*.

6. The first thing they do is choose a shape for the button. They then type in a name for the button. Suggest they use words such as *Click Here*. The text is typed into the *Name* box. Now students can choose the color of the text and background of the button. They can click on any of the colors in the color boxes. Finally, students should click *OK*.

7. Explain that after they click *OK* the button appears on the card. To move the button, students should click on the button and drag it where they want it. Then they should click anywhere on the screen to add the button actions.

8. Now students will need to decide where the user will go when he or she clicks on the button (usually the next card). In the *Places to Go* box select *Next Card* by clicking on the button next to *Next Card*. Now, students need to choose a transition. The transition is what happens as the card disappears and the next card comes onto the screen. Students can choose any transition, then click *OK*.

9. Students also need to add a sound to the button. Tell them they should click on *Play a Sound* in the *Things to Do* box to choose any sound. If they want to hear the sound, they should click on *Play*. When they are finished, they should click *OK* and then click *Done*. Students should follow the same procedure to add buttons on the next cards.

10. To add their second card, students click on the *Edit* menu and select *New Card*. On the second card, students use the paint tools to draw a map of the state and add a button to move to the third card.

11. On the third card, students list tourist attractions. They draw an illustration of one or more places, as well as add descriptive text. Add a text box by clicking on the *Objects* menu and selecting *Add a Text Box*. A text box will automatically appear on the card. To move the text box, students click on the box and drag it where they want it. Then they click anywhere on the screen to format the text appearance.

12. Tell students that they will not be naming the text box so they should not type anything in the *Name* box. They should pick a color for the text and background of the text box. They can click on any colors in the color boxes.

13. Students won't be typing much text, so they don't need a scrollable box. Therefore, tell students to unselect *Draw Scroll Bar* and *Scrollable* by clicking on the check marks to remove them. The boxes should not be checked.

14. Students format the text by clicking on *Style*. They can choose any font, style, size, and alignment for the text. Then, they click *OK*. Students immediately type in the text. When they are finished, they add a button to move to the fourth card using the same procedures explained earlier.

15. The fourth card includes a picture of the state bird, state flower, and a button to move to the fifth card.

16. The fifth card contains a text box with information on the elected officials of the state. If you want to further challenge students, ask them to include those elected to both houses of Congress. To finish, instead of choosing *Next Card*, students should choose *Another Card*. Then, they should use the arrows to find the first card in the stack. When they reach the first card, they should click *OK*. This will "loop" the stack.

17. Students test their stacks by clicking on *Move* and selecting *First Card*. Then they go through their entire multimedia presentations to be sure all the buttons work correctly.

18. When students are finished, they save the file as **state.their initials**.

19. Remind students to quit or exit the program when they are finished so that the computer is ready for the next student.

20. You may want to review the steps on the activity card with students so that they can work independently at the computer.

21. If you have a large-screen projection device, have students use this to share their multimedia presentations with the entire class.

Assessment Criteria

1. Presentation contains at least five cards.

2. Student presented accurate information.

3. Student looped presentation correctly.

4. Student used tools correctly.

State Report

1. Open the *HyperStudio* program.

2. Use the paint tools to draw a graphic that represents the state you selected. Type the name of the state and your name on the card.

3. Add a button by clicking on the *Objects* menu and selecting *Add a Button*.

4. Choose a shape and name for the button. The name of the button should be typed into the *Name* box.

5. Choose the color of the text and background of the button. Click on any of the colors in the color boxes. Click *OK*.

6. Move the button by clicking on the button and dragging it where you want it. Then click anywhere on the screen to add the button actions.

7. In the *Places to Go* box, select *Next Card* by clicking on the button next to *Next Card*. Choose a transition and then click *OK*.

8. Add a sound to the button. Click on *Play a Sound* in the *Things to Do* box. Then choose any sound. If you want to hear the sound, click on *Play*. When you are finished, click *OK* and then click *Done*.

9. Add your second card by clicking on the *Edit* menu and selecting *New Card*. Use the paint tools to draw a map of the state and add a button to move to the third card, following the same procedures explained earlier.

10. On the third card, add information about sites to see. Draw an illustration of one or more sites along with text describing the best sites.

State Report (cont.)

11. Add a text box by clicking on the *Objects* menu and selecting *Add a Text Box*. A text box will automatically appear on the card. To move the text box, click on the box and drag it where you want it. Then click anywhere on the screen to format the text appearance.

12. Don't type anything in the *Name* box. However, you should pick a color for the text and background of the text box. Unselect *Draw Scroll Bar* and *Scrollable* by clicking on the check marks to remove them. The boxes should not be checked.

13. To format the text, click on *Style*. Choose a font, style, size, and alignment for the text. Then, click *OK*. Immediately type in the text. When you are finished, add a button to move to the fourth card, following the same procedures explained earlier.

14. The fourth card should have a graphic of the state flower and state bird and a button to move to the fifth card.

15. The fifth card should have a text box with information on the elected officials of the state and a button to move back to the first card. Instead of choosing *Next Card*, choose *Another Card*. Then, use the arrows to find the first card in the stack. When you reach the first card, click OK. This will "loop" the stack.

16. Test your stack by clicking on *Move* and selecting *First Card*. Go through the entire multimedia presentation to be sure all the buttons work correctly.

17. Save the file as **state.your initials**.

18. Quit or exit the program.

FS123298 Making the Most of the One-Computer Classroom © Copyright Frank Schaffer Publications, Inc.

reproducible